B I R D S
OF GRAND TETON NATIONAL PARK
And The Surrounding Area

BY BERT RAYNES

D1010361

BIRDS

OF GRAND TETON NATIONAL PARK
And The Surrounding Area

BY BERT RAYNES

FOR MEG RAYNES

and

Nipper
Jenny
Misty
Hilary

© 1984 Photographs by
Dan Abrams, Erwin and Peggy Bauer,
Franz Camenzind, Jeff Foott, Jackie Gilmore, Leo Larson,
Thomas D. Mangelsen, Edward A. Riddell, Jon Stuart.

© 1984 Text by Bert Raynes

Published by Grand Teton Natural History Association

Project Coordination by Sharlene Milligan

Photo Editing, Book Design, Typography and Production by Riddell Advertising & Design

Text Editing by Debbie Broaddus

Lithography by Paragon Press

First Printing, 1984
Second Printing, 1989

ISBN 0-931895-00-6

FOREWORD

Sometimes I think I have read as many books on birds as I have seen species of birds. The books tend to fall into two categories. One category is best described as highly scientific, useful for accurate identification, and difficult to read for enjoyment. Other books seem to fall into a second category of pictures with extended captions that could have been written by anyone with knowledge of birds or of books in the first category, but lacking an understanding of the local avifauna and associated enjoyment opportunities. In other words, bird books seem to be either for the serious bird fanatic or for the browser with a passing interest in birds.

What we have here is a book that I can't categorize. But then that is to be expected. I defy anyone to categorize the author, Bert Raynes. It is a book for the browser as well as useful to the bird fanatic. More importantly, it will be most useful for the majority of us who just want to enjoy birds by learning more about new species or familiar species in different situations without the threat of cerebral overload.

In the Jackson Hole area, 293 species have been recorded. Over twenty-six of these species have never been or only rarely recorded in other areas of Wyoming. These records partly reflect the unique opportunities to observe birds in this area, but also reflect the author's success in locating birds and encouraging others to observe and report birds.

This book features sixty species that have obviously been carefully chosen. The featured species will give the reader a good cross section of common species, the "high profile" birds; the unique species for which one has as good or better chance of observing in the Jackson Hole area as anywhere else in the United States; and some of Uncle Bert's favorites. This cross section gives serious birders, novices, or the experienced hobbyist, a decisive head start on enjoying and learning more about the avifauna of this unique area.

BOB OAKLEAF
Non-game Bird Biologist
Wyoming Game and Fish Department

ACKNOWLEDGMENTS

First, and foremost, I enthusiastically acknowledge my gratitude to Meg Raynes, superior wife, and superior birder when she wants to be. She could not co-author this book as I had hoped, but she has been supportive of and has made more enjoyable most of my birdwatching pleasures by sharing in them. I am of course grateful to many fellow birders and friends as well. Specific to this book I am pleased to mention: Erwin and Peggy Bauer, whose encouragement to publish something like this volume was pivotal; Sharlene Milligan and the Board of Directors of the Grand Teton Natural History Association; Ed and Lee Riddell of Riddell PhotoGraphics; Bob Oakleaf, Non-game Bird Biologist, Wyoming Game and Fish Department; Dave Lockman, Waterfowl Specialist, Western Wyoming, Wyoming Game and Fish Department; Bob Wood, Resource Specialist, Grand Teton National Park; Patrick Smith, Chief Naturalist, Grand Teton National Park; Dan Abrams; Eddie Bowman; Katy Duffy; John Wilbrecht, Project Manager, National Elk Refuge; Frank Craighead; Fred Kingwill; Ernie Abeles; Mary Lohuis; and all the members and friends of the Jackson Hole Bird Club. I am sorry all of the great bird photographs submitted by so many fine wildlife photographers could not have been selected, but I am enormously flattered by the quality represented.

Not to forget the naturalists who have studied and published on birds in northwestern Wyoming and the many professional and amateur birdwatchers who have made their observations a matter of record. In recent years many visitors to the area have completed and mailed a Jackson Hole Bird Checklist; their contributions enable that compilation to be refined and made increasingly reflective of what a birder may hope to see, and in what season.

Fashions by King Size Inc. Transportation by sluggish V.W. All notes and manuscripts on recyclable materials.

Thanks, too, to the birds.

BERT RAYNES
Jackson Hole, 1984

TABLE OF CONTENTS

INTRODUCTION

This book offers help to the casual or intense birdwatcher in finding many of the birds that occur in Grand Teton National Park and the surrounding valley and mountains. Not every bird will be found on any given day at the sites specified. Birdwatching is, as are all attempts to observe nature, full of temporary disappointment. It is also full of surprise, enlightenment, and enjoyment. It is a sport, and a challenge, and a chance to see wild creatures doing the incredible feats they are capable of without overt self-consciousness.

Habitat is the basis for the recommendations of where to see the birds featured in this book. A full page map keyed to the specific sites and habitats mentioned is provided at the end of the habitat section. Each page in the bird section has a small map which is color-coded to the habitats in which the species is likely to be found. The seasons during which some species may be expected in the region are suggested, along with a written description. Also described are birds similar in size, plumage, or habitat selection that could possibly be confused for the species sought. To further help the birder, a photograph representing each species accompanies its description. All of these photographs were taken by local wildlife photographers.

While you may not see the bird you seek in a given place, you may instead see a bird rare to Grand Teton National Park. Or you may see a bird at a time when its presence is unexpected. Your written record will be most helpful in expanding the knowledge of bird behavior and occurrence in the Park. A bird checklist similar to the one reproduced in this book can be obtained at Park Visitor Centers and at other federal and state agencies in the region. Please fill it out and drop it in the mail; postage is provided. These records are earnestly solicited.

The habitats in and surrounding Grand Teton National Park are unusually variable, ranging from rich riparian to sparse alpine. Birds will be seen everywhere within the region—no matter how sedentary or active you are. There is no obligation to know precisely what species any bird is—a big black bird is description enough for a Common Raven, fundamentally. But many find putting names to birds and flowers and trees and stars to be satisfying and enjoyable. This book is aimed at those in that category, with the hope that it will bring pleasure.

UNCLE BERT

HABITATS

SEVEN MAJOR BIRD HABITATS

Here is the Teton Range, rising without foothills over a mile above the flat valley known as Jackson Hole, and forming its western boundary. To the north and east of the valley are the Yellowstone Plateau and the Mt. Leidy Highlands. The southern end of the valley is enclosed by the Snake River Range, and the Gros Ventre and Hoback Mountains.

The valley floor has an average elevation of about 6,500 feet above sea level. Many of the surrounding mountains rise above tree line, over 10,000 feet above sea level, and the Grand Teton itself reaches to 13,770 feet. A major river, the Snake, bisects the "hole."

The Jackson Hole area includes seven major bird habitats; all are represented within the boundaries of Grand Teton National Park. These habitats encompass a large freshwater lake, Jackson Lake; the valley floor; many miles of the Snake River and its tributaries and their flood plains; and the surrounding mountainsides, including the steep glacier-carved eastern slopes of the Teton Range.

With the exception of the private land upon which homes, businesses, and ranching operations occur, most of the valley outside the Park and most of the mountainsides are federally administered. These public lands include portions of the Bridger-Teton National Forest and the National Elk Refuge. It therefore happens, happily for the birdwatchers as for all people, that almost all of this dramatically beautiful land is accessible.

The following descriptions will help orient the visitor, birder or not, to the region's seven primary habitat zones: Riverbottoms; Lakes and Ponds; Sageflats; Ranches and Hayfields; Morainal and Piedmont Forests; Mountainsides; Alpine Zone; and Settlements.

RIVERBOTTOMS

Jackson Hole extends about fifty miles from north to south and about twelve miles from east to west at its widest point. The boundaries of Grand Teton National Park contain about 60 percent of the valley floor. The Snake River flows through the entire valley in a southwesterly direction. Three other major rivers run into the valley from the east and are tributaries to the Snake: the Gros Ventre River near the center of the valley; the Buffalo Fork in the north; and the Hoback River at the extreme southern end.

To the birdwatcher, these rivers and their tributary waters are important. Many bird species utilize streams and riverbottoms at some time during each year and live, nest, and forage there. Birds such as Yellow Warbler, Willow Flycatcher, Barrow's Goldeneye, and Bald Eagle are found in this habitat.

Narrow-leaf cottonwood trees and blue spruce grow immediately along the rivers, interspersed with grassy areas and willow swamps. Silverberry, honeysuckle and chokecherry form the understory. Access to this habitat is generous. It may be reached by paved highways, by trail, and by rivercraft.

© LEO LARSON

LAKES AND PONDS

The first impoundment of the wild Snake River occurs where the Jackson Lake Dam has enlarged a natural lake. Jackson Lake dominates the northern end of the valley and attracts many of the bird species found in this entire region. At the north end of Jackson Lake and adjacent to the dam structure, cobble shoreline gives way to mud flats where waterfowl and shorebirds gather in season. In contrast, Jenny Lake and other morainal lakes at the base of the Teton Range are deep, cold, and relatively devoid of aquatic plants and thus are not so attractive to water-specific birds. Ponds and lakes to the east of the Tetons, such as Christian Pond and Two Ocean Lake, and those in the other mountains enclosing Jackson Hole are far more productive for the bird student. Birds such as Canada Goose, White Pelican, California Gull, and Peregrine Falcon may be found on or near the lakes and ponds.

The forests and openings surrounding the lakes and ponds are rich in birdlife. One may find Northern (Red-shafted) Flicker, Gray Jay, Pine Siskin, Red Crossbill, and White-crowned Sparrow.

Access to the eastern shore of Jackson Lake is by paved road, trail, and a variety of watercraft. The numerous smaller lakes and ponds throughout the region are reached mostly by trails or dirt roads. Some, such as Two Ocean Lake in Grand Teton National Park and Slide Lake in the Gros Ventre Mountains, are reached in summer on good roads.

© EDWARD A. RIDDELL

SAGEFLATS, RANCHES, AND HAYFIELDS

This important bird habitat covers large areas of the valley floor. Vegetation is a mixture primarily of sagebrush and bitterbrush, along with some native grasses. In places irrigation has altered this glacial outwash plain into lush hayfields and cattle ranches. Many birds use and require this habitat, but birding it will often demand patience and some luck. Even a little fortitude, since dawn is the best time of day to find Sage Thrasher, Vesper Sparrow, and Sage Grouse.

Many miles of both paved and unpaved roads traverse the sage flats. In this respect, access is relatively easy to achieve on the federally administered lands. Private ranchlands should not be trespassed upon; however, permission to birdwatch is often given when ranching operations permit. Casual birdwatching in the National Elk Refuge is limited to established unpaved roads.

© FRANZ CAMENZIND

MORAINAL AND PIEDMONT FORESTS

This habitat exists from the valley floor to approximately 8,500 feet above sea level. Above the sagebrush flats and at the base of the mountains are dense forest stands. These are primarily coniferous forests, with some stands or individual clones of quaking aspen. On the eastern slopes of the Teton Range are morainal forests comprised primarily of lodgepole pine, Engelmann spruce, subalpine fir, and Douglas fir, along with a few aspen, growing upon glacial debris. These forests attract a variety of birds quite different from those preferring the cottonwood-spruce habitat of the riverbottoms. Here nest Western Tanager, Great Gray Owl, and Chipping Sparrow.

Unlike the Teton Range, other mountains of the region have foothills and thus have more typical piedmont forests where quaking aspen is more common among lodgepole pine and where stands of spruce and fir are irregular. In these surrounding mountains, north-facing slopes are more heavily forested than south-facing hillsides, which in turn are sometimes entirely unforested. This diversity attracts a wider variety of birdlife, which includes Hairy Woodpecker, Yellow-rumped Warbler, Mountain Chickadee, Ruffed Grouse, and Red-tailed Hawk.

Many miles of trails in Grand Teton National Park and of unpaved roads in the surrounding mountains penetrate this habitat. The highways over Teton and Togwotee passes and going to Yellowstone National Park all go through stretches of this region. Access is relatively easy.

MOUNTAINSIDES

This habitat lies from 8,500 to 10,500 feet above sea level. Above the morainal and piedmont forests and up to treeline, spruce-fir forests grow among rock outcroppings and on talus slopes. Lodgepole pine disappears and quaking aspen occurs only in infrequent stands; subalpine fir, Douglas fir, and Engelmann spruce are the dominant conifers. Whitebark pine stands and alpine meadows are found. Bird species in this mountainside habitat are relatively few but include some of the region's vertical migrants: Pine Grosbeak, Steller's Jay, Gray Jay, Clark's Nutcracker, and Golden Eagle.

This habitat is more difficult to reach than are some others. After the ground dries, say in June, unpaved forest roads are passable, some by passenger vehicles. Foot and horse trails go up to this interesting habitat in Grand Teton National Park and in the Bridger-Teton National Forest. In winter, access may be gained on skis or showshoes and on snowmobiles where permitted. The highway over Teton Pass reaches 8,400 feet; Togwotee Pass is 9,600 feet above sea level.

ALPINE ZONE

This habitat exists above tree line, about 10,500 feet above sea level and up. In the Teton ecosystem, isolated stretches of terrain are above tree line. This is a harsh habitat, where winds blow hard, where large daily temperature fluctuations are experienced, where vegetation is sparse and alpine flowers and shrubs have only a few weeks in which to reproduce. To reach this habitat, one has to earn it the hard way, on foot or on horse. The sole exception is a tram that runs from a base station in Teton Village to a station above tree line on Rendezvous Mountain in the Tetons just south of the National Park boundary. Passengers are taken during summer and in winter to an elevation of 10,050 feet.

In the Alpine Zone only a few species of birds are to be found. Two species nest there: Rosy Finch and Water Pipit. Other birds visit, including Peregrine Falcon, Tree Swallow, Golden Eagle, and Common Raven.

SETTLEMENTS

Towns, developments, and ranches in Jackson Hole and housing areas in Grand Teton National Park and Bridger-Teton National Forest exert an influence on birds and all other wildlife of the region far beyond their physical dimensions. The major settlement and business district, the town of Jackson and its immediate environs, is located toward the southern end of Jackson Hole. There, at the lowest elevations, snowfall is the lightest in the region so snow cover seldom completely hides food sources from wintering birds for extended periods.

Winters in this location in the northern Rocky Mountains are exceedingly long and usually harsh. As one result, few resident birds or birds in spring or fall migrations will fail to investigate the plowed roads or streets, the road edges, and the sheltered places—and the birdfeeders—in Jackson, the towns of Kelly and Wilson, the recreation area of Teton Village, and the government housing areas in Moose and east of Moran. At any time of year, in fact, the settlements should be included in the birdwatcher's itinerary. Access is easy, by car, on foot, or on a horse or a bicycle.

Summer birding in the settlements can be rewarding: Yellow Warbler, Western Wood Pewee, Evening Grosbeak—even American Dippers sometimes nest. Winter birding will turn up Rosy Finch (Black and Gray-crowned), Clark's Nutcracker, Townsend's Solitaire, Pine Grosbeak, and Dark-eyed Junco. On any given day it is possible to look above the towns and see a Bald Eagle, perhaps a flight of Canada Geese, or a family of Trumpeter Swans.

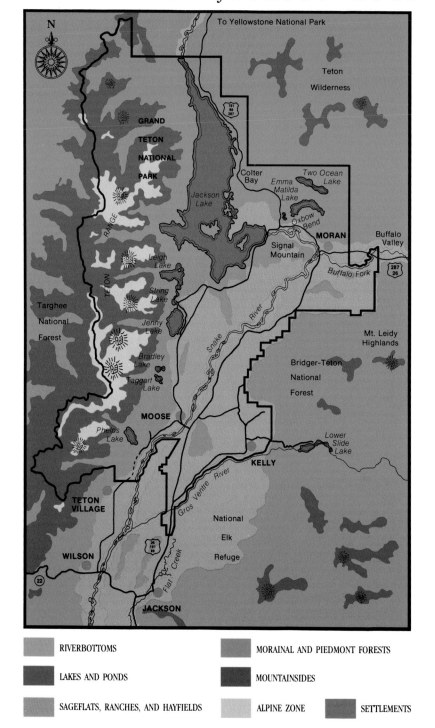

RIVERBOTTOMS

MORAINAL AND PIEDMONT FORESTS

LAKES AND PONDS

MOUNTAINSIDES

SAGEFLATS, RANCHES, AND HAYFIELDS

ALPINE ZONE

SETTLEMENTS

BIRDS

© THOMAS D. MANGELSEN

COMMON LOON
Gavia immer

BEST BET
The Common Loon is an open water bird. Jackson Lake near the dam, Two Ocean Lake, Jenny Lake, and the Oxbow are the only waters in the area which seem to attract it regularly.

COMMENTS
This is a big black and white bird, up to three feet in length. It sits long and low in the water, head down. The Common Loon can submerge by changing its density and slipping under water, but generally dives powerfully. It was once called the Great Northern Diver because it usually stays under for thirty seconds or longer and is known to dive to two hundred feet. It fishes but can do well on aquatic vegetation, insects and other non-fish energy sources.

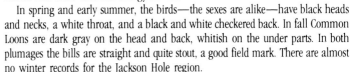

In spring and early summer, the birds—the sexes are alike—have black heads and necks, a white throat, and a black and white checkered back. In fall Common Loons are dark gray on the head and back, whitish on the under parts. In both plumages the bills are straight and quite stout, a good field mark. There are almost no winter records for the Jackson Hole region.

The Common Loon presently nests only on a few small lakes in the extreme northern reaches of the area. Detailed maps will show a Loon Lake in the area north of Grand Teton and south of Yellowstone National Parks. It probably nested on Two Ocean and Emma Matilda Lakes in Grand Teton, but increased human pressure on these lakes presently prohibits nesting. In late fall, however, the wonderful wild yodeling howls can sometimes still be heard, and on even rarer occasions echoing on Jackson Lake.

LOCAL
LOOK-ALIKES
The Arctic Loon is smaller and has a thin straight bill. It closely resembles the Common Loon, but has a gray—not black—head. The Double-crested Cormorant is a large, all black, water bird. It has a low swimming profile, as do loons, but has a hook-tipped bill. Cormorants frequently stand erect on rocks or tree stumps, often holding their wings out to dry.

WESTERN GREBE
Aechmophorus occidentalis

BEST BET | Jackson Lake, especially in fall. Occasionally found on other lakes in the region.
COMMENTS | Grebes are water birds, diving birds, once thought to be related to loons. The Western Grebe is the largest grebe in North America. With its long, swanlike neck and needlelike bill, with its ability to remain underwater for long periods, and with its black and white pattern, it does resemble a loon. The Western Grebe is black on its upper parts, and the white is confined to the long neck. It is an alert, almost regal-looking bird—characteristics a couple of other, much smaller grebes share—and always looks, somehow, clean.

Western Grebes occur in two color phases. The face pattern in the dark phase bird shows black on the head extending below the eye to the bill, whereas in the light phase bird the black cap is always above the eye. The dark phase Western Grebe apparently predominates in Grand Teton National Park, although at least one light phase bird has been documented. Reports of birds of either phase will be appreciated.

LOCAL | Loons are black and white and also superb swimmers and divers, but they are
LOOK-ALIKES | short-necked, even lumpy in appearance.

©JEFF FOOTT

AMERICAN WHITE PELICAN
Pelecanus erythrorhynchos

BEST BET
In late spring, summer, and fall it will be found, if anywhere, on Jackson Lake, on the Oxbow, or flying along the Snake River.

COMMENTS
The White Pelican is a bird of the interior lakes of western America. A huge bird, among the largest on the continent, it is fifty to seventy inches in length and up to twenty pounds in weight; the adult has a wingspread of eight to nine and a half feet. It is white with black tipped wings, has an enormous orange or salmon-colored bill, and orange-red feet and legs. (The White Pelicans found in and near Grand Teton National Park are probably non-nesting birds.)

The White Pelican flies easily and well, with powerful—and audible—wing strokes and alternating glides. It often soars to great heights and delights in aerial acrobatics. It swims lightly, feeding—usually in groups—on fish. The White Pelican DOES NOT dive for fish as does its relative the Brown Pelican of the oceans.

These huge white birds nest in colonies on the ground, usually on islands, and in this overall ecosystem on the southern arms of Yellowstone Lake in Yellowstone National Park, where powerboating is restricted. According to anecdotal records, they once nested on Jackson Lake.

LOCAL
LOOK-ALIKES
There are other large birds that can be mistaken for the American White Pelican. The Trumpeter Swan has no black in its wings. The Whooping Crane has black in its wings but flies with its neck extended and long legs trailing. The American White Pelican flies with its head hunkered back on its shoulders and with its long flat bill resting on its breast. Pelican flocks fly in orderly patterns, each bird alternating several flaps with a glide. The Snow Goose is small in comparison, and has a small bill.

GREAT BLUE HERON
Ardea herodias

BEST BET

Riverbottoms, lakes, and ponds. The Oxbow, Blacktail Ponds, South Park, all along the Snake River and its tributaries, the upper Gros Ventre River and its tributaries. Spring, summer, fall. A few birds winter over.

COMMENTS

The Great Blue Heron is a great big bird. The adult stands four feet tall and has a wingspan of six feet. In flight, its neck is held in a graceful S curve with its head folded back against its shoulders, and its legs are extended behind. Making its living eating fish, aquatic insects, frogs (even mice or ground squirrels), it is readily found at water's edge or in the shallows. It stands either with alertly extended neck or in a hunched over posture. At other times it can be seen stalking elegantly.

The Great Blue, as it is affectionately called, is almost unmistakable, and it is often observed in Grand Teton National Park and surroundings. Its large size and its silhouette in flight are distinctive. It is gray-blue-dark in most lights—but some adults do have lighter colored heads, tending toward white. The large bill is sharply pointed. The voice in flight is a harsh, gooselike *honk;* if the bird is startled, it is a gutteral, short *squark.* Great Blues nest in colonies, each pair making a substantial, if untidy, platform, in conifer and cottonwood trees in this region. In summer, when the young are being fed (by both male and female parent), Great Blues may be abroad at any hour of the day or night.

LOCAL
LOOK-ALIKES

The Sandhill Crane is also a long-legged, tall bird found in Grand Teton National Park and its environs. The Crane also has a six-foot wingspread. In flight, however, the Sandhill's wings are *flicked* upwards (rather than swept downwards, as in the herons) and the neck is held outstretched. The Sandhill is uniformly gray or brownish except for red on the bare skin of the head. The Sandhill Crane is a bird of the marsh, wet grasslands, and sagebrush. The Great Blue prefers water.

© *THOMAS D. MANGELSEN*

TRUMPETER SWAN
Cygnus buccinator

BEST BET Christian Pond in primary nesting season. The National Elk Refuge/Flat Creek in fall, winter, and spring. Buffalo Valley.

COMMENTS The Trumpeter Swan is the largest of the North American waterfowl. It is huge. It can be found in this region all year, almost exclusively on watercourses on the valley floor. During the most severe winter weather, when temperatures reach forty degrees below zero and lower, the swan depends upon warm springs and a few sections of major rivers or creeks. Fairly tame birds, a few pairs become so accustomed to people that they nest and reside where they can be easily observed.

In the middle of this century, the sanctuary of the greater Yellowstone ecosystem preserved a small Trumpeter Swan population of perhaps four hundred birds—all the remaining birds in the lower forty-eight states. Efforts continue in order to encourage their well-being. As a result, some swans may be sporting neck collars, marked to permit biologists to monitor their progress. Please report such birds to the authorities; your observations can be helpful in preserving the species.

LOCAL LOOK-ALIKES Tundra (Whistling) Swan and Snow Goose occur regularly in the region in early fall and winter. American White Pelican, in flight, can also be mistaken for Trumpeter Swan but it has black wing tips. The Trumpeter Swan has a low-pitched, brief *beep* call. The call of the Tundra Swan is higher pitched and musical, resembling the Canada Goose call. The Snow Goose call is a still higher pitched falsetto. American White Pelican is silent except near breeding grounds, some of which can be found on Yellowstone Lake in Yellowstone National Park.

© THOMAS D. MANGELSEN

CANADA GOOSE
Branta canadensis

BEST BET — Lakes small and large throughout the Grand Teton National Park ecosystem, where they breed. On many of the sand bars in the Snake River. Ranchlands and grassy areas, where they graze. In fall, large concentrations are found on Jackson Lake, where they persist almost until freeze-up in December. Also look on Christian Pond, the Oxbow, Swan Lake, and at the National Elk Refuge.

COMMENTS — Without doubt, the best known wild goose is the Canada Goose. It is big, standing up to two and a half feet tall. It migrates both day and night in noisy V-shaped flocks.

Pairs of Canada Geese will frequently nest close to human activity, and in the southern part of the Jackson Hole area goslings will appear as early as the first week of May—when the northern extremities are still frozen over and Park trails are two months from being open.

The Canada Goose is gray-brown, with a black head and neck, a *white* cheek, and a light-colored breast. The bill and legs are black. The "honker" that occurs in Grand Teton National Park and surrounding regions is the Western Canada Goose *(B. canadensis moffitti)*, one of the largest of the ten recognized forms.

LOCAL LOOK-ALIKES — Unlikely to be mistaken for any other waterfowl on the water or on the land. The silhouette in the air resembles all the geese, but the steady V-flights usually accompanied by the familiar deep *honk* should be specific.

© ERWIN AND PEGGY BAUER

MALLARD
Anas platyrhynchos

BEST BET Riverbottoms, river edges, small piedmont ponds and lakes. Christian Pond, Two Ocean Lake, in the shallows of the Snake River, the National Elk Refuge, in ponds and puddles in the Bridger-Teton National Forest.

COMMENTS The Mallard is a big common duck. It's tough and adjustable. The Mallard is one of the "puddle-ducks"; that is, it feeds on the water by dabbling and "tipping-up" without diving. The male has a smooth gloss-green head, a narrow but distinct white neck band, and a chestnut breast. Moreover, its generally gray body ends in a white tail with upcurled black central feathers. In flight, prominent white borders on both sides of the purple-blue speculum (an iridescent patch on the trailing edge of the wing) can usually be seen. If that's not enough, add a yellow bill, and bright orange feet. Kinda snazzy.

The female is the same size—two feet in length or more—but mottled brownish and dark-billed. Feet are also orange, and the white-bordered speculum and whitish tail help to identify her. Female Mallards quack, in a descending series. Drakes make a softer note.

Mallards are mostly seedeaters, going after sedge and grass seeds, sometimes seeds of bottom land trees, and grains. Don't be too surprised to find them on a golf course, on a gravel bar in a large river, or in an irrigation ditch.

LOCAL LOOK-ALIKES Male Shoveler ducks have a dark head with a green sheen, but the bill is large and shovel-shaped, and since the chest is clear white, the white neck collar of the Mallard is lacking. Red-breasted Merganser males have heads glossed with green, are rusty-chested to the waterline, and have a side white neck collar. But their heads are crested, and their bills and feet are red. Female Pintails resemble female Mallards, but are sleeker and have white borders only on the rear edge of the lackluster speculum. Female Pintail bills are gray, not black or orange. Female American Wigeons superficially resemble hen Mallards but have gray heads, a white speculum, and are smaller and more slender.

© THOMAS D. MANGELSEN

CINNAMON TEAL
Anas cyanoptera

BEST BET Riverbottoms, lakes, and ponds. Christian Pond, Swan Lake, Two Ocean Lake, the Oxbow, National Elk Refuge. Shallow bodies of water, small reservoirs, even irrigation ditches.

COMMENTS The male Cinnamon Teal is a tiny, but handsome, shallow-water duck. It is a uniformly rich dark mahogany or cinnamon color on body and head and has a large cerulean-blue patch on the leading edge of the wing. The female Cinnamon Teal is comparatively nondescript: it has a sporty blue wing patch but is otherwise a foot-long patchy brown little duck. In fact, the female cannot be told in the field from the female Blue-winged Teal, its close relative; but since interbreeding does not seem to occur frequently, a female with a male Cinnamon Teal can be presumed to be of that species.

There are three species of teal in Grand Teton National Park and its surroundings: the Cinnamon, the Blue-winged, and the Green-winged. All jump directly into the air when alarmed, a characteristic of so-called surface feeding puddle ducks. Their flight is usually low and twisting, and appears to be more rapid than it actually is. Cinnamon Teal and Blue-winged Teal usually fly in tight groups; Green-winged Teal are more loosely allied, often following one leader.

LOCAL LOOK-ALIKES The male Blue-winged Teal has a large, white crescent on its head in front of the eye and a white patch on the body near the tail, but it also has a bluish wing patch. The male Green-winged Teal has a white mark on the body in front of the wing and a lemon-yellow patch near the tail. In good light, an iridescent green patch on the side of the head can be seen, as can a green patch on the secondaries of the wings. The Ruddy Duck is small and reddish, the male in breeding plumage has a blue bill, it has white on the cheeks in all plumages, and it is a diving duck. It will often dive rather than fly from danger. Ruddies often cock their tails jauntily; teal do not.

© THOMAS D. MANGELSEN

BARROW'S GOLDENEYE
Bucephala islandica

BEST BET The Snake River, Flat Creek, Christian Pond, the Oxbow; many smaller ponds and lakes, especially on the valley floor.

COMMENTS This diving duck is found in the Grand Teton National Park area and its surrounding waters all year long. Courtship begins early, usually in February, and is fun to watch, including as it does feather puffery, rapid head and body movements, and glimpses of the drake's brilliant orange feet. The male Barrow's Goldeneye is black and white and sports a glossy purple, evenly rounded head. There is a white *crescent* in front of the eye—all in all, quite a dapper, jaunty bird. Both Barrow's and Common Goldeneyes occur in this region and it is quite difficult to distinguish between the females of this species. In courtship, the bill of a breeding female Barrow's Goldeneye becomes very yellow, usually all yellow. The bill of the female Common Goldeneye is black with a distinct yellow tip. The best way to identify them, though, is to see which males they are with; there is little evidence of hanky-panky in these species.

These ducks nest in hollows of trees—usually near a small pond or stream but sometimes surprisingly distant—and now and then under brush or even under a rock. The Goldeneye is our "whistler duck," a nickname derived from the high pitched whirring noise made by its wings in rapid, direct flight. This "song" identifies the bird as one or the other of the Goldeneye species.

LOCAL LOOK-ALIKES The Barrow's can easily be mistaken for a Common Goldeneye, and vice versa. The male Common Goldeneye has a large *round* white spot in front of the eye, and at close range its head is seen to be glossy greenish. Two other black and white diving ducks are somewhat similar in appearance to the Barrow's: the Common Merganser—but it has no facial patch and is long and low; and the Scaup—but it has a black chest and prefers the larger waters of Jackson Lake.

COMMON MERGANSER
Mergus merganser

BEST BET   National Elk Refuge, the Oxbow, Jackson Lake, Jenny Lake, Two Ocean Lake, Snake River. Riverbottoms and lakes.

COMMENTS   The Common Merganser is a long, slim, big duck, which flies in follow-the-leader formations, low over the water, low over winding streams. The male is largely white with a greenish-black head and a black back; at close range, it can be seen that the breast is tinged with a light rufous color. The female Common Merganser is gray-bodied with a crested, bright reddish head and neck. She has a definite white throat patch *within* the red of the neck. Males are white at the water line; females are grayish. The Common Merganser is one of the largest of all the ducks that can be found in Grand Teton National Park and the surrounding waters and marshes.

Common Mergansers can be found all year long in the area. Families of these sleek birds can be seen often on Jackson Lake and other lakes in the area, as well as on the big rivers. Nesting sites are widely variable, from tree cavities to ground locations to old hawk or raven nests in the timber.

LOCAL LOOK-ALIKES   The male Goldeneye, Barrow's or Common, is stubbier, with a large head and distinct white eye spots. The female Red-breasted Merganser, which occasionally occurs here in spring and fall on migration, resembles the female Common Merganser, but its head is a paler rufous color, its chest is dingy, and its white chin is not as sharply outlined. Best to check out the males. Canvasback and Redhead Ducks have black chests and no crests. The male Mallard, also a big duck, has a green head.

© FRANZ CAMENZIND

O S P R E Y
Pandion haliaetus

BEST BET Riverbottoms, lakes, and ponds. Jackson Lake, especially the west shore. Along the Snake River, from roadways or from rivercraft. Along the Buffalo Fork and the Gros Ventre River.

COMMENTS This large, dark brown and white hawk eats fish almost exclusively. The way it catches fish is a spectacular affair: from a height of up to one hundred feet, the Osprey hovers, then falls feet-first into the water, wings half-closed. The fish, once seized in the bird's talons, is secured. With effort, the Osprey rises from the water, shakes, streamlines the fish by arranging it headfirst, and flies off to a feeding perch or to its nest.

In ordinary flight, the Osprey is recognized by its size—two feet in length and with a wingspread of four and a half feet—and by a characteristic crook or backward sweep of the wings. The Osprey is white below and dark brown above; it resembles an eagle and is often mistaken for one. Its call is a series of sharp, high-pitched whistles, very loud and, once learned, distinctive.

Ospreys are conspicuous nesting birds in Grand Teton National Park and its adjacent waters. Usually the nests are in trees, dead or living, and are used year after year, until they become too large. Sticks, clods of earth, and sometimes just debris are brought to the nest, mostly by the male. In a few places in the region, pairs of Ospreys have used power poles as nesting sites for many years.

LOCAL LOOK-ALIKES Sometimes a Bald Eagle will force an Osprey to give up its catch; at these times the difference in size between these two raptors is apparent. The wings of adult Bald Eagles are very broad and entirely black. An Osprey's tail is banded, not entirely white. The Rough-legged Hawk has a dark belly and shares black "wrist" marks with the Osprey. Rough-legged Hawks usually arrive in winter, when Ospreys are leaving, and they leave the Grand Teton National Park area when Ospreys return in spring.

BALD EAGLE
Haliaeetus leucocephalus

BEST BET Usually near water, in this region primarily along the Snake River, so a river trip should be rewarding. Jackson Lake, the Oxbow, Moose. In November, Bald Eagles follow the elk migration south from Yellowstone National Park to the National Elk Refuge.

COMMENTS The mature Bald Eagle is impressive: all-white head; broad, black wings spreading up to eight feet across; black body; all-white tail. When in soaring flight, the enormous wings are held horizontal, and the eagle may sometimes cross from horizon to horizon without a single flap. Bald Eagles still nest in Grand Teton National Park and south along the Snake River, close to their major food supply, fish. A few nests are in the National Forests adjacent to the Park, and there are several out of the area, south along the Snake River.

The future of the Bald Eagle in the Grand Teton National Park environs, as in the nation as a whole, is the subject of considerable concern. Bald Eagles that nest within the Park and some of the other federal lands are given some protection. Efforts are made to maintain zones of little or no human activity near them. Eagles that nest on private lands are being crowded by human activities, particularly housing developments, and their continued presence, not to mention nesting, is in doubt. These birds must not be harassed in any manner, and, as are all the birds described in this book, they are protected by federal law.

LOCAL LOOK-ALIKES The Golden Eagle is a great broad-winged bird of prey. The adult Golden is uniformly dark, with a wash of gold on the head and neck. *However,* the immature Bald Eagle may be confused with the Golden Eagle; it is easy to mistake immatures of either species for the other. Immatures can look so much alike that a good field guide is a necessity. The Osprey is a fish-eating hawk, also dark brown and white. But it is much smaller and has a distinctive black line on its white face.

© THOMAS D. MANGELSEN

SWAINSON'S HAWK
Buteo swainsoni

BEST BET
Fence posts on open ranching areas in the sagebrush from the Buffalo Valley south to the southern extremity of Jackson Hole. In open aspen stands. Moran, Kelly, and south of Jackson.

COMMENTS

A soaring hawk, about the size of a Red-tailed Hawk, Swainson's Hawk has distinctive and unusual *dark* flight feathers. This is the best field mark, even when a confusing melanistic, or dark, bird is involved. The tail is long and the wings are pointed and long, distinguishing it from other buteos. There are two phases found in Grand Teton National Park and surrounding open country. One phase has a dark breast, pale wing linings, dark flight feathers, and a gray tail shading to white at the base. The dark, or melanistic, phase bird has a darkish body and wings, but the tail is usually barred with gray.

The Swainson's Hawk commonly hangs about highways looking from fence posts and power poles for dead animals or unsuspecting live ones. Its principal food, the ground squirrel (in this area, the Uinta ground squirrel), seems at times to be incapable of keeping off the roads, and many of these little mammals—known locally as "chiselers"—are killed by vehicles.

This is a particularly attractive buteo, or soaring hawk. It shares hunting territories with the Red-tailed Hawk and will sometimes be seen in serious aerial combat with one during their overlapping nesting seasons. The Swainson's has a rather forlorn, almost cat-like call. The Red-tail has a wild squealing call, rather fierce.

LOCAL LOOK-ALIKES
The Red-tailed Hawk has a dark head, a light chest and some belly streaks, along with its short red tail. The Rough-legged Hawk has clear white on its flight feathers. A hunting Swainson's Hawk often flies low with wings raised in a open V, as does the Northern Harrier (Marsh Hawk), which is slim, has a white rump patch, and whose flight appears to be unsteady.

THOMAS D. MANGELSEN

RED-TAILED HAWK
Buteo jamaicensis

BEST BET
In every habitat. Look near ranchland south of Jackson, all along the Gros Ventre, Buffalo, and Snake Rivers, and south of Moran in the large meadows.

COMMENTS
The Red-tailed Hawk is a large, soaring hawk. A female will have a wingspan of four and a half feet and be almost two feet in length. Red-tail wings are quite broad, and this feature is accentuated by a relatively short, wide tail. The tail is, of course, reddish, but usually only on its upper surface; below it is without color in both adult sexes.

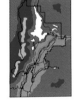

Naturally a Red-tail can't fly all the time. Perched, it looks short-tailed and thick, and often chooses the top of a dead tree. Perching posture usually is upright. Red-tails make a wild, harsh squeal or hiss, oddly weak for its size and line of work.

Red-tailed Hawks will take prey ranging from rodents, to birds, to reptiles, to insects, not excluding carrion. This lack of specialization, and a willingness to nest on cliffs, in big timber, or in low trees in open country, accounts in part for its wide distribution.

LOCAL LOOK-ALIKES
A bunch. Bob Oakleaf has a few tips on separating Red-tailed Hawks from Swainson's or Rough-legged Hawks:
1) Red-tails tend to have a dark head, light chest, dark belly body pattern.
2) Swainson's often have a dark head but a white throat area, or dark breast and a light belly body pattern. Flight feathers on Swainson's are dark.
3) Rough-legs have light heads, sometimes heavily streaked dark bellies, and also have white in their tail as well as in their flight feathers.

If you are going to get at all serious about hawk identification, you will need all the field guides you can carry. There is a lot of variation in each species. There are light-phase birds, dark-phase birds, there are differences in tail feathering and in wing linings. And that's in adult birds. Immatures are even tougher. The chances are overwhelming that you will say, at least at times, "that looks like a something-or-other hawk." Even an expert, perhaps even Oakleaf, gives up on some birds.

© THOMAS D. MANGELSEN

AMERICAN KESTREL
Falco sparverius

BEST BET Along streams such as Fish Creek; and the Snake, Gros Ventre, Hoback, and Buffalo Fork rivers. On National Elk Refuge fences, and on powerline poles in the sagebrush areas. In and around Kelly and Moran.

COMMENTS The American Kestrel (formerly Sparrow Hawk) is the smallest falcon in North America. The male is shorter than a ten inch long Robin and the female is only an inch longer. Falcon's wings are, however, long and slender and come to a point, so the Kestrel's two foot wingspread and its swift flight create an impression of a significantly larger bird.

The Kestrel prefers open country, which it hunts often from a vantage point such as a powerline pole or wire, or a tree top. It hovers a great deal, too, as it hunts; this is excellent field behavior to recognize. Insects, especially grasshoppers—even ants— form a large part of the diet in season. Small mammals and birds are taken.

Both sexes have a striking black and white face pattern, and rufous on their backs and tails. The female's tail is banded with black; the male's is tipped with black. Male Kestrels also have blue-gray wings. Kestrels sit erect and exhibit the falcon silhouette of large head, broad shoulders, long wings and long tail.

The Kestrel is a showy bird, exciting as a falcon always is. It is wary of man, but will nest close to him, sometimes even in niches in buildings. The *klee-klee-killy-killy-klee* call is high-pitched, rapid, and wild.

LOCAL LOOK-ALIKES The Merlin (or Pigeon Hawk) is about the same size as a Kestrel and has a falcon's pointed and shaped wings. The Merlin does not have rufous on its back or tail, and does not have a facial pattern. It has a banded gray tail in the male, brown in the female. The Sharp-shinned Hawk is an accipiter, has rounded wings, and is gray or brown on its back.

© ERWIN AND PEGGY BAUER

PEREGRINE FALCON
Falco peregrinus

BEST BET The cliffs of the Teton Range, and the large water areas of the region; this is the Duck Hawk. The western shore of Jackson Lake, near the many canyon mouths flanked by steep rock walls, during the nesting months of June, July, and August.

COMMENTS In 1970, the Peregrine Falcon, one of the most magnificent of all birds, was almost gone forever from the contiguous United States, a victim of indiscriminate use of persistent pesticides. This was an almost unbelievable fate for a bird that has coexisted with man for at least four centuries and was once considered one of the most successful of all birds.

Some of the best Peregrine Falcon habitat in Wyoming, as determined by historical evidence and direct observation, is in the Grand Teton National Park area. Beginning in 1980, efforts to reintroduce Peregrines were begun. With the continuation of the release of young birds each summer and the chance that surviving breeding age birds will establish nests somewhere in the miles of suitable habitat here, there are again chances to see Peregrine Falcons in the Teton Range.

This Crow-sized falcon, with its long, pointed wings, compressed tail, blue back, dark, boldly patterned head and contrasting paler undersides, is simply exciting to see. It is an extremely agile and swift falcon, capable of spectacular aerial maneuvers—soaring, thousand-foot dives, twists and turns. Its prey is mostly birds, knocked right out of the air by a blow from the falcon's foot. Or the Peregrine may just pick its prey up in its feet on the fly. The Peregrine can catch a Swift and it chases the Golden Eagle; where the Peregrine lives, the Peregrine is the boss bird.

Please report any observations of Peregrines, with as much detail as possible, to the Wyoming Game and Fish Department, or to Grand Teton National Park.

LOCAL LOOK-ALIKES The Prairie Falcon is the same size as the Peregrine, but the Prairie is pale, brownish-tan and lacks the black hood. The Prairie Falcon has blackish patches where the wings join the body. The Merlin (Pigeon Hawk) and the Kestrel (Sparrow Hawk) are Robin-sized, not Crow-sized.

PRAIRIE FALCON
Falco mexicanus

BEST BET
Rough, dry country, lower elevation canyons, and open mountainsides. In and around the National Elk Refuge, on Blacktail Butte, around the Mt. Leidy Highlands, and near Moran.

COMMENTS
The Prairie Falcon is a handsome, sleek, twenty-inch long, pale brownish-tan, pointed-wing bird of prey. In flight it shows blackish patches where the wings meet the underbody, in its armpits as it were; the single best field mark. Look quick . . . few birds fly faster and this falcon often flies right on the deck, perhaps twenty-five feet above the ground or lower.

Prairie Falcons hunt ground squirrels, small birds and even grasshoppers. Their close relative, the Peregrine Falcon, which again occurs in the region, takes small mammals on occasion but specializes in taking birds. Peregrines occur in the Teton Range and into Yellowstone National Park because of a program which began locally in 1980 to reintroduce this species. Once again both Prairie and Peregrine Falcons can be expected to be found in this region in spring, summer, and fall. The Wyoming Game and Fish Department, The Peregrine Fund, and Grand Teton National Park will be grateful for your reports of both species.

LOCAL
LOOK-ALIKES
The Peregrine Falcon is the same size as the Prairie, a bit smaller than a Crow, but has a blue back and a dark, patterned head—it appears to sport a black hood with sideburns. Merlins (Pigeon Hawks) and American Kestrels are Robin-sized falcons.

BLUE GROUSE
Dendragapus obscurus

BEST BET   Morainal and piedmont coniferous forests. In spring in open grassy areas; in late fall and in winter Blue Grouse go higher, up to near tree line at times. The west shore of Jenny Lake, on the trail from String Lake to and along Leigh Lake, Signal Mountain near its summit. Blue Grouse seem to prefer the south end of the Jackson Hole area.

COMMENTS   In spring, a male Blue Grouse might come up to you on the trail and nip at your blue pants or aqua-colored backpack. Or you might walk up on one that is strolling across an open glade in the piedmont forests or perhaps find one sitting close to the trunk of a conifer. You may hear one hooting, a deep note difficult to pinpoint. You will probably have to be alert; these "fool hens" are expert in camouflage and can disappear from view in a few paces. If you do spot one you might be able to approach carefully and observe it at quite close range.

What you will see is a sixteen inch long, blackish, chicken-like bird, if it is a male. Both sexes have distinctly *black* tails, but the female Blue Grouse is otherwise gray-brown. The adult male has a yellow-orange patch of bare skin above the eye. Grouse, considering how tame they are, can be surprisingly difficult to identify. Even the experienced birder will want to take care to note all the field marks.

LOCAL LOOK-ALIKES   The Ruffed Grouse is a gray-brown or sometimes slightly reddish bird whose reddish-brown tail has broad black *bands* near the tips. The Ruffed Grouse drums in courtship, whereas the Blue Grouse gives a series of five to seven hooting calls. The female Blue Grouse resembles the female Ruffed Grouse.

The Spruce Grouse does not appear to occur here, even accidentally, although its range comes close to the Grand Teton National Park ecosystem. Any sightings of Spruce Grouse—a black grouse with white spotting on its sides—would be of importance to the naturalists of the region.

SAGE GROUSE
Centrocercus urophasianus

BEST BET — Strictly on the sagebrush flats. For most of the year it is chancy. One must stalk the sagebrush near dawn. In early spring—late April, first part of May—on the ancestral courtship grounds: one such lek is on the north end of the present-day Jackson Hole Airport runway; others are along US 26 north and south of Moose, near the intersection with the Kelly Road; and several are near the town of Kelly. In some late winters, along the Kelly Road and near the Kelly Warm Springs.

COMMENTS — Sage Grouse are not numerous in the sagebrush flats of the region, but the spring courtship display makes up for the relative scarcity. At that season, the male Sage Grouse, large and colorful, really struts its stuff, rapidly inflating and deflating its yellowish breast air sac and making a loud *blooping* sound, spreading its pointed tail feathers into a fan that arcs over 280 degrees. It dances with mincing steps on feathered legs, puffing out its chest, sticking out its black belly. In addition, the male "Sage Chicken" sports a black throat and yellow eye combs. No wonder the drab, much smaller female, which has only the dark belly, is impressed. In recent years, Grand Teton National Park has reinstated a dawn automobile trek to witness Sage Grouse courtship on the Jackson Hole airport runway at favorable times; the observations cease when air traffic commences. These tours are advertised annually, normally coming sometime between April 15 and May 15; it depends on how the juices are flowing.

Sage Grouse are harder to find during the rest of the year, but they may appear anywhere in sagebrush. These birds are game birds in most of the rest of Wyoming and are very much more common to the south of Grand Teton National Park—say fifty miles south, near the town of Daniel.

LOCAL LOOK-ALIKES — The Sage Grouse is big; the male is twice the size of the other grouse found in the area. The female is grayish and shows the distinct black belly. A big, turkey-like bird, flying powerfully and then sailing for a long distance over the sage plains, is pretty surely a Sage Grouse.

© JEFF FOOTT

AMERICAN COOT
Fulica americana

BEST BET In spring, American Coots prefer shallow ponds and marshes; go to the National Elk Refuge, Christian Pond, Swan Lake. In summer and fall, look there but also look on creeks and deeper water; Flat Creek in the National Elk Refuge; Jackson Lake, Two Ocean Lake.

COMMENTS The American Coot looks like a duck, swims like a duck, dives like a duck, and even quacks (sometimes) like a duck, but it is in the same family of birds as Rails and Gallinules. It is not a duck; it is, in fact, related to Cranes.

The Coot is a water bird, but will sometimes feed on land. Most of the time it tips for food, as puddle ducks do, but it can dive, like a loon or a grebe. It cannot rise directly into flight, but must run over the water, often for quite a distance. Swimming motion is distinctive, as the bird nods or pumps its head and neck vigorously back and forth. It is a gray-black bird with a small black head and a small *white* bill; there is a small white patch under its tail.

American Coots nest in the Grand Teton region by the dozens and migrate through in the spring and, especially, in the fall, often in the thousands. Rafts of Coots are common on Jackson Lake in fall, almost until freeze-up in December.

The American Coot is a kind of "plain-Jane" bird—dirty black with a touch of white on each end—weaving and bobbing through life without undue fear: it does not taste good to people so it isn't hunted. The chicks are something else. They are black downy little characters except for flamboyant curly bright red hairs all over their heads and necks. Unexpectedly charming.

LOCAL LOOK-ALIKES The American Coot resembles a duck. The small black body, the white bill, and the nodding motion of the head as the bird swims identifies this species.

SANDHILL CRANE / WHOOPING CRANE

Grus americana / Grus canadensis

BEST BET Sandhill Cranes nest in Grand Teton National Park and its surrounding reaches, in marshes and fields: Willow Flats, National Elk Refuge, ranches south and east of Grand Teton National Park. In current years Whooping Cranes of the new New Mexico-Idaho flock have been migrating through the area, and one bird has summered for two years in the Buffalo Fork drainage.

COMMENTS Both of the cranes that are found in the western United States can be found here; the Sandhill Crane nests, and the Endangered Whooping Crane is now being seen.

The Sandhill Crane is a large bird, standing almost four feet tall and having a wingspan of six to seven feet. The adult is light gray in color, long-legged, long-necked, with a bald red crown. The young Sandhill is brown, lacking the red.

Cranes have a distinctive striding walk and a distinctive wing motion in flight, a rapid upward flicking beat of wings that never drop below the body line. Cranes migrate in groups, sometimes very large flocks, sometimes flying at great heights. At these great heights the Sandhill can look quite whitish.

The all-white Crane with the red face is the Whooping Crane; a large, four and a half foot tall bird with huge, black-tipped white wings that span seven and a half feet. The story of this endangered bird has been well publicized. An effort to create a flock of Whooping Cranes that will nest in and around Idaho and winter in or near New Mexico is underway; Whooping Cranes seen in Grand Teton National Park and its environs are from this project, which is headquartered in Grays Lake National Wildlife Refuge, about eighty airmiles from Park Headquarters.

LOCAL LOOK-ALIKES The White Pelican is a large white bird with black on its wings, but it flies with its neck pulled in. The Great Blue Heron flies with legs trailing, as the Crane does, but with its neck pulled in also. The Snow Goose is far smaller and its legs and feet do not extend past the tail.

Although the Sandhill Crane in flight can sometimes look whitish, the Whooping Crane is unmistakably, always, WHITE.

© DAN ABRAMS

KILLDEER
Charadrius vociferus

BEST BET Mostly on the riverbottoms and along adjacent elevations, wet and dry. All along the Snake River and other watercourses, including pond and lake edges. However, Killdeer can also often be found on plowed ranchland and on road gradings. The extensive dikes along portions of the Snake River are heavily used for nesting. Some birds will winter over, along the Snake River especially.

COMMENTS The scientific specific name for this showy shorebird, *vociferus*, is certainly apt. The Killdeer definitely is. A loud *kill-dee, kill-dee* is given during all times of the year. This little plover also gives a querulous *dee-dee-dee, dee-dee-dee* and, mostly in nesting season, a long trill.

The Killdeer is an orange-brown robin-sized bird, about ten inches in length, including its rather long tail. This wading bird has two dark brown bands across its clear white breast. In flight the long tail extends past a reddish rump, and each wing displays a prominent white stripe. The flight is swift and graceful, even buoyant.

This is one bird species that you probably cannot overlook. It is an alert bird, and one of its duties seems to be warning all other birds of any intruder with its cries and its short flights. The Killdeer also does one of the best "broken-wing" acts in the business when its nest and young are approached.

LOCAL LOOK-ALIKES The Semi-palmated Plover is smaller and has only one breast band or ring. Two Killdeer-sized plovers that are much less common to this region, the Black-bellied Plover and the American Golden Plover, do not have clear breasts in any plumage. In flight the Killdeer resembles a small falcon, and can be mistaken for the American Kestrel.

© THOMAS D. MANGELSEN

SPOTTED SANDPIPER
Actitis macularia

BEST BET There is probably no stretch of water, running or still, below tree line that isn't a potential spot at which to see the Spotted Sandpiper. Found along the Snake River, the shores of Jenny and Jackson Lakes, Christian Pond, the Oxbow, Slide Lake, and along Spread and Pilgrim Creeks.

COMMENTS In its breeding plumage this little wading shorebird is aptly named; no other sandpiper has round black spots on its underparts, neck to tail. In fall and winter the spots are lost, and this little seven inch shorebird becomes quite inconspicuous—olive-brown above, whitish below. A white line over the eye, a white spot on the shoulder just above the bend of the wing, and the pale yellow base of the lower mandible help to identify this little "peep" in this plumage.

Far easier, regardless of the time of year, is identification by habits. The "Spotty" constantly bobs its tail up and down as it walks on rocks or logs near water—it is the "teeter-tail" of the birds. The Spotted Sandpiper flies in a distinctive flutter on stiffly held, *down-curved* wings; its wings appear not to rise above the bird's lower body. The call is a series of *peet-weets* or a long series of *wheet* notes. Or it can be a single whistle, like a spring peeper's.

This sandpiper can perch on branches or wires, will swim underwater, or will even walk on the bottom like a dipper.

LOCAL LOOK-ALIKES A half dozen other small sandpipers are found in this high mountain valley environment, but none of the others teeter as they walk or fly with the downwardly held, stiff wings. The Spotted Sandpiper prefers rocky or pebbly shorelines, rather than mud flats.

© THOMAS D. MANGELSEN

COMMON SNIPE
Gallinago gallinago

BEST BET — Wet places in the lower elevations and the piedmont streams and ponds. National Elk Refuge, irrigation ditches on the ranchlands, marshy areas along the river edges, mud flats on Jackson Lake, pastures and wet plowed fields.

COMMENTS — The Common Snipe is a short-legged, short-necked, long-billed, brownish, medium-sized sandpiper with a strongly striped head and back. The head stripes go *along* the head. In flight the bird's long, pointed wings and short, orangish tail are evident.

The Common Snipe generally "freezes" when startled, hanging tight and depending upon protective coloration for security. A bird may rise almost at your feet, giving a short rasping *jaack* note and zigzagging quickly away, more than likely scaring the dickens out of you. It may also sit on a fence post, in full view, and let you approach quite closely, if you will take your time. Far more often it is heard, and not seen, as it flies its eccentric circles high in the sky and then makes a sudden dive that causes "either its wings or its narrow outer tail feathers to vibrate and produce a high-pitched, pulsating hum or whistle" (Richard Pough). This noise is ventriloquial and carries well. Produced on a cloudy day or late in the evening or early in the morning, its origin can be puzzling. It is one of the wonderfully wild sounds in nature.

LOCAL LOOK-ALIKES — The Woodcock is very rarely seen in the Grand Teton National Park region. Its head is also striped, but the stripes run *across* its head. Its wings are short and rounded, not pointed.

The Long-billed Dowitcher also has a long bill and looks a lot like a snipe. The Common Snipe likes wetlands; the Dowitcher prefers open mud flats.

THOMAS D. MANGELSEN

WILSON'S PHALAROPE
Phalaropus tricolor

BEST BET   Shallow ponds and marshes, even transient wet areas in meadows and pastures. Mud flats on Jackson Lake, Christian Pond and the Oxbow, marshy areas on the National Elk Refuge, on ranchlands and near settlements.

COMMENTS   The female Wilson's Phalarope is a beautiful shorebird. In this species (and in the two other Phalaropes in North America) the female has the more brilliant plumage; can't imagine what went awry in this bird's evolution. The nine inch long female is richly colored, with "a broad face-and-neck stripe of black blending into cinnamon" (Roger Tory Peterson). Wings are long and thin and uniformly dark with wing stripes visible only in flight. Also in flight, the rump patch is white and the tail is whitish. Males are duller, have a white spot on the back of the neck, and a pale chestnut wash on the side of the neck. Bills are black and sharply pointed.

Wilson's Phalaropes swim buoyantly but very often feed where they can wade, picking insects wherever detected. Another characteristic of this species is its spinning in the water when feeding. The birds will spin "like tops" while rapidly dipping their bills into the riled-up surface water for food. Another good field mark of this graceful bird is its habit of holding its wings upright for a moment upon alighting either on water or on the mud flat or shallow wet area.

LOCAL LOOK-ALIKES   The Northern Phalarope is a similarly sized and shaped shorebird but is gray above with a white throat patch and red on the neck. It does not have neck stripes.

Lesser Yellowlegs has dark wings and a white rump but is larger and bulkier. In flight, of course, the yellow legs are diagnostic. Bills are not quite as needle-like.

© THOMAS D. MANGELSEN

CALIFORNIA GULL
Larus californicus

BEST BET
Jackson Lake, especially where fishermen return with their catches, such as Colter Bay, Signal Mountain boat ramp, Leek's Marina, or just below the Jackson Lake Dam. Two Ocean Lake, Christian Pond, along the Snake River. Gulls are strong fliers and can occur anywhere in the region.

COMMENTS
If you want to see a California Gull and can't seem to locate one, carry a fishing rod to some fishing access almost anywhere along the riverbottoms, Jackson Lake, or the lower elevation piedmont ponds or lakes. If one is around, it will probably find you and look you over. Catch a fish and go to clean it and the gull may just let you see all its field marks.

The California Gull has a white head, body, and tail, with gray upper wings and upper body. Wing tips, seen from below, are sharply black with white at the outer extremities. The wing tips and the red—or red and black—spot on the bill are excellent field marks. Legs are a greenish color. This gull is about twenty inches in length. It is not always easy to identify gulls, even those that can be seen readily and are at close range, so look for all the marks.

The California Gull is the most common gull in the region, but not the only one. It is the most common because it prefers to nest inland, not on the coasts. California Gulls descended by the thousands to eat the long-horned grasshoppers (the Mormon Cricket) that threatened to destroy the crops of the early Mormon pioneers in Utah. A monument to this gull is a landmark in Salt Lake City today.

LOCAL
LOOK-ALIKES
Oh my, yes. Those "sea-gulls" are discouragingly similar. The Ring-billed Gull is smaller than the California (about eighteen inches). It has a complete black ring all around the bill and is a paler overall gray.

There is a cult that claims to be able to distinguish easily among young gulls in the field. True believers may be able to.

© THOMAS D. MANGELSEN

GREAT HORNED OWL
Bubo virginianus

BEST BET
Riverbottoms and piedmont forests. Scout the brushy cottonwoods and aspens. Owls are not predictable. Look around Moose, Colter Bay, and around the towns of Jackson and Wilson.

COMMENTS

The Great Horned Owl is an "eared" owl. It is a large—females are two feet long—fierce, no-nonsense bird of prey. The prey can be fish, rodents (especially mice and voles), rabbits, birds (even Red-tailed Hawks), domestic cats, and, not to overlook any gourmet item, skunks.

The Great Horned Owl is heavily barred, dark brown-gray underneath, a more uniform coloration on the back. It has a conspicuous white throat, but seems not to have a neck, which accentuates the large appearance of the head. It is mostly nocturnal, but on overcast days it will be seen in the afternoon.

The Great Horned Owl calls in a series, usually three to eight, of deep, deceptively soft *hoo* notes. These birds are exceptionally early nesters, and their hooting is given frequently in late February through April. If you should hear one scream, you are unlikely to ignore it.

LOCAL
LOOK-ALIKES
The Long-eared Owl is similar, but it is *much* smaller (a little over a foot in length) and is streaked *lengthwise* underneath. The Long-eared Owl is gray, with a rusty face.

©JEFF FOOTT

GREAT GRAY OWL
Strix nebulosa

BEST BET In the timber adjacent to meadows. The morainal and piedmont forests seem to be preferred, but the Great Gray Owl will also be found in riverbottom cottonwood/-spruce stands. Since it hunts often in daylight, the Great Gray Owl sometimes perches in an exposed conspicuous position adjacent to the forest and can be approached closely. Try around Moose and the Colter Bay campgrounds.

COMMENTS The Great Gray Owl is the largest owl in North America; it is twenty-four to thirty-three inches long, including a foot long tail. It has a five foot wingspread. The head looks almost too large for its body, and the yellow eyes and facial discs with concentric circles further emphasize the head size. There are no ear tufts on this all-grayish owl. Adults appear to sport a mustache.

The Great Gray Owl prefers pocket gophers and voles as prey, along with other small rodents that are seldom seen above ground in broad daylight. Thus, the owl is abroad in early morning and late afternoon. As a result it is seen more often than are many other owl species.

Adult Great Grays give deep booming hoots. Young birds screech and whistle. These fascinating birds are not infrequently seen in the region, but their appearance is unpredictable. A sighting is quite exciting, even for experienced birders, for these owls are considered rare almost everywhere on the continent. Reports of sightings will be appreciated.

LOCAL None, really.
LOOK-ALIKES

© JEFF FOOT

COMMON NIGHTHAWK
Chordeiles minor

BEST BET All along the Snake River, Blacktail Ponds, along the upper Gros Ventre River, Jackson Lake Dam, and the Willow Flats. Primarily a summer resident, migrating south in September.

COMMENTS  The Common Nighthawk is only about ten inches long, the same length as a Robin, but always appears bigger in flight. This is probably due to the two foot wingspread and long, pointed, falcon-shaped wings with conspicuous white patches near the wrist, away from the wing tip. The Nighthawk strongly resembles a falcon as it hunts the sky for flying insects. Its flight is more erratic or variable than a falcon's and it usually utters a distinctive nasal *peent* call at frequent intervals. During courtship, the male Nighthawk makes a faintly rude, booming sound with its wings as it pulls up after a fast earthward dive.

Nighthawks are brownish gray, and the male has lighter areas on the tail and under the chin. But most identifications are made by shape, action, call, and the large white wing bars. These graceful birds nest in the Grand Teton National Park area, but actual reports of nests are lacking. Should you find one, in "simple depressions" on gravelly soils or in a burnt-over portion of open forest, please notify a Park Ranger, a biologist, or a local birder.

LOCAL LOOK-ALIKES The Poor-will occurs only accidentally in the area; it is smaller and has no white on the wings. The Nighthawk looks like a small falcon but is usually active at sunrise and at dusk, when falcons are usually inactive. The Nighthawk will hunt at all hours, even all night on occasions.

©JEFF FOOTT

CALLIOPE HUMMINGBIRD
Stellula calliope

BEST BET   The Willow Flats, willows along streams, feeders in Jackson and other settlements. July and August are the best months. Among patches of blooming scarlet gilia.

COMMENTS   The Calliope Hummingbird is the smallest bird in Grand Teton National Park and for a long way. It is suspected to be the smallest bird in the United States. A Calliope may be only two and three quarters inches long, from tip to tail, and will probably never be more than three and a half inches. And these hummers weigh almost nothing—less than a tenth of an ounce.

Hummingbirds are difficult to identify not only because they are so small but also because they fly so fast, because females and young of most species are almost identical to the eye, and because the best field marks, the throat feathers of the males, are iridescent and in poor light they are featureless. Four of the fifteen North American hummingbirds occur here; the Calliope is the most common. The male Calliope Hummingbird has purple-red *streaked* feathers on a white throat; this is diagnostic.

Hummingbirds hover, fly backwards or forwards, are aggressive towards one another, and move their wings so rapidly that individual wing beats cannot be distinguished by the human eye. It may be enough just to enjoy watching them feed on flower nectar and interact with each other, and not make too many demands on species identification.

LOCAL LOOK-ALIKES   Broad-tailed Hummingbird wings make a distinctive shrill metallic noise, and the male has a *solid* red throat offset by a green head. The Black-chinned Hummingbird has a truly black throat—in all lights—a green and black head, and a purple upper chest patch. The male Rufous Hummingbird has a solid reddish head and back and a brilliant red throat patch.

The hummingbird moth strongly resembles a tailless hummingbird as it flutters, but the beats of its wings can be individually distinguished as the insect sips nectar.

BELTED KINGFISHER
Ceryle alcyon

BEST BET Almost wherever there is water. Flat Creek, shallows of the Snake and Gros Ventre Rivers, along the shoreline of Jenny and Jackson Lakes, along all the valley's smaller streams. Resident, unless no open water can be found in winter.

COMMENTS The Belted Kingfisher's wild, loud, rattling call is one of nature's finest sounds, not to be mistaken, not to be forgotten. It is given either as the bird is perched or when it is swooping past, flying low and alternating a series of five or six wing beats with long glides.

It is called the Belted Kingfisher because of the blue-gray band across the breast of the male and the two bands, one gray and one rust, on the female (the female is the more colorful of this species). Easier to spot than the banded breast are the big head with its unruly, rakish crest and the big sharp bill. The Belted Kingfisher is a big bird, larger than a Robin. It is mainly a fish eater, but will eat mice, insects, and even wild fruit. The Kingfisher hunts by night as well as by day, using favorite perches— whether willows, cottonwoods, evergreens, or electric power lines—over-hanging water. From these perches it dives headlong into the water, most often emerging with a fingerling.

LOCAL LOOK-ALIKES Can't think of one.

© THOMAS D. MANGELSEN

HAIRY WOODPECKER
Picoides villosus

BEST BET Found everywhere except the alpine heights and the sagebrush and bitterbrush flats. All the trails in the Park and forests are good possibilities. Walk around Jenny Lake. Teton Village and Jackson usually have several pairs all year long.

COMMENTS The Hairy Woodpecker is a large—eight and a half to ten and a half inches—flashy black and white forest bird. Look for the clear white back, black wings with a few white spots, and a large, chisel-shaped bill. The male Hairy Woodpecker has a small bright red patch on the back of its head. The breast is clear white.

The Hairy Woodpecker feeds preferentially on the larvae of tree-boring beetles and nests in holes it excavates in living or dead trees. Its flight is distinctively undulating, a characteristic of all woodpeckers. Its note is a loud, sharp, emphatic, single *peek*, quite attention-getting. A descending rattle of notes is also given. Woodpeckers "sing" by pounding a resonant tree limb; the Hairy's song is loud and slow.

LOCAL LOOK-ALIKES The Downy Woodpecker looks just like a small Hairy Woodpecker; clear white back, black wings with spots, clear breast; the male has a small red head patch. The bill is *much* smaller; this and the six inch length are its best distinguishing features. The Downy Woodpecker note is a sharp, soft *pik* and its "song" is long and rapid.

The Three-toed Woodpecker has a white or a ladder back and barred sides. The male has a yellow cap, no red at all.

© ERWIN AND PEGGY BAUER

THREE-TOED WOODPECKER
Picoides tridactylus

BEST BET Morainal and piedmont forests. Areas of coniferous forests that have been newly and severely burned will, in the first spring following the fire, echo with the hammering of Three-toed Woodpeckers—and with the gnawing of flat headed wood-borers. Otherwise, expect irregular sightings where dead conifers with peeling bark are plentiful. Try the Leigh Lake Trail.

COMMENTS The (Northern) Three-toed Woodpecker and its companion species, the Black-backed (Three-toed) Woodpecker, are not well understood. They come from who knows  where and by routes known so far by no one, to nest and forage in newly-burned conifer forests. Their population in such forests is highest the first year following a burn and falls off sharply thereafter, returning in half a dozen years to "normal" population levels. In Grand Teton National Park and environs, there may normally be only a handful of Three-toed Woodpeckers and Black-backed Woodpeckers.

It is easier to see the yellow caps on male Three-toed Woodpeckers than to count their toes. These are both robust, relatively large woodpeckers. The Black-backed has a solid black back set off by barred sides. The Three-toed, more common here, has either a white or a barred back. Normally, no other woodpecker to be found in Grand Teton National Park will have a yellow cap.

LOCAL LOOK-ALIKES Similarly sized woodpeckers can be mistaken for the Three-toed Woodpecker, especially, of course, the Black-backed Woodpecker. The Black-backed has a solid black back and barred sides. Males have a yellow cap. The female lacks the yellow cap and, except for her barred sides, resembles the Hairy Woodpecker.

Williamson's Sapsucker, either male or female, may easily be mistaken for the Three-toed Woodpecker; but Sapsuckers are far more common in the region. The Sapsucker male has white shoulder patches and a red throat patch; the female has a zebra-back, barred sides, and a brown head.

© ERWIN AND PEGGY BAUER

NORTHERN FLICKER
Colaptes auratus

BEST BET Riverbottoms and morainal and piedmont forests. Widespread and common. Prefers deciduous trees. Around Moose, Colter Bay, and on trails in Jenny and String Lake areas. In Jackson, Wilson, Kelly, and Moose.

COMMENTS The Northern (Common, Red-shafted, Yellow-shafted) Flicker is a large *brown* woodpecker with a showy white rump that is readily visible during its undulating flight. The underwings and tail are a rich salmon-red: the red shafts. The male has a red mustache.

Flickers are noisy. The note is a loud *klee-oo*. The call is *flick-a*, given in a long series. In nesting season, sometime in May and June, they drum loudly on a hollow tree limb, a metal sided or metal roofed house or shed, or even a traffic sign. If you happen to be inside such a house and ready for sleep or perchance romance, your reaction to this drumming may not be one of affection returned.

In the Grand Teton region, Northern Flickers often stage spring and fall migrations, in which many hundreds participate.

LOCAL
LOOK-ALIKES The Yellow-shafted Flicker form is rare in this locality and can be distinguished by its bright *yellow* under-tail and wing shafts. Both flickers commonly feed on the ground, usually eating ants, but also go for other insects and wild fruits.

The female Williamson's Sapsucker is a brownish woodpecker and has a white rump. The female also has a yellow belly, a zebra-striped back and barred sides, and a warm brown head. Williamson's Sapsuckers are usually found on trees, not on the ground, and are only about two-thirds the length of the foot-long Northern Flicker.

© *THOMAS D. MANGELSEN*

WESTERN WOOD-PEWEE
Contopus sordidulus

BEST BET Found along the rivers, in aspen clones and open deciduous woods, in conifers, around houses in the trees, and halfway up the mountains. Gros Ventre Campground, Jackson Lake shoreline, Signal Mountain, and in the towns of Moose and Jackson.

COMMENTS The Western Wood-Pewee is one in the family of birds called Flycatchers or Tyrant Flycatchers: aggressive, almost exclusively insect-eating, songbirds. It is a large family—thirty-five species are found in the United States. In the Jackson Hole area, nine or ten species can be seen or heard. Some small Flycatchers are so similar in appearance that unless they do sing, even big-time bird books say they cannot be reliably identified in the field.

The Western Wood-Pewee can be distinguished. It is a generally dark gray-brown little bird, about six inches long, lighter on its belly, and it has *no*—or at best an indistinct—eye ring. It does have two white wing bars on each wing. It does flycatcher things: catching insects in mid-air, darting out from an exposed perch to which it often returns after securing its prey, with an audible—a kind of satisfied—click of its bill if the insect was small enough. Large insects are carried back to a perch and torn into bite-sized pieces.

The Western Wood-Pewee's song is rather harsh, a penetrating and carrying nasal *pee-er*. This penetrating note may be given all day and into dusk, uttered so often it might not be distinguished from insect trills and buzzes unless specifically listened for.

LOCAL LOOK-ALIKES Too many. It is possible to find five of the Empidonax Flycatchers in Grand Teton National Park and its general ecosystem, and all can be confused with the Western Wood-Pewee. Unlike the Pewee, however, these five all have distinct light-colored eye rings. They are: Willow, Least, Hammond's, Dusky, and Western Flycatchers. The Olive-sided Flycatcher is larger and seems to prefer the tips of dead trees, from which it loudly calls "Quick! Three Beers!!"

© THOMAS D. MANGELSEN

CLIFF SWALLOW
Hirundo pyrrhonota

BEST BET This swallow likes the unforested portions of the region. Teton Village and the other settlements are good bets, as are outbuildings in the ranches of the area.

COMMENTS The Cliff Swallow has an almost *square* tail, an excellent field mark. It also has a pale red rump, a dark throat patch, and a creamy white or tan forehead.

This is the "mud swallow" of the region; it carries small mud balls in its beak and constructs its nest from them on cliff faces, on the sides of buildings, and under bridges. Both sexes build the nest, creating a bottle-shaped bowl with a narrow side-tube entrance. Sometimes, when the clay isn't of good "throwing consistency," the nests become simpler, just a soupbowl. Either way, these remarkable structures get pretty full when there are four or five active youngsters crowded inside.

On the wing or at the nest, Cliff Swallows chatter constantly, making a series of low *chur* sounds and another that sounds a lot like a creaking gate hinge. They are colonial nesters, and present a cheerful, busy sight where they congregate. What they are busy about is catching insects, their exclusive food. Hurrah!

LOCAL LOOK-ALIKES All swallows are fast fliers, agile and graceful. The *Violet-green* Swallow has white rump patches that almost meet over the base of the tail and it is greenish and purple on the back, clear white below. It tends to be in the forests and along the rivers. The *Tree* Swallow is blue-black above, clear white below. The *Bank* Swallow is brown on the back and has a dark breast band on an otherwise clear breast. The *Rough-winged* Swallow is brown on the back but has no breast mark. The *Barn* Swallow has a deeply forked tail.

These species often intermingle when feeding or migrating. After a while, the species can be separated by appearance, flight pattern, and voice. Honest.

©*THOMAS D. MANGELSEN*

G R A Y   J A Y
Perisoreus canadensis

BEST BET Campgrounds, trail heads, wherever humans congregate and scavenging can be had. In winter, also to be found in settlements: Jackson, Moose, Kelly, Moran. Permanent resident in forests of the valley floor, the moraines, and the mountainsides.

COMMENTS Camprobber. Whiskey Jack. Meat Bird. Lumberjack. Canada Jay. And now Gray Jay. This is one of the best known birds in the northern reaches of the continent and throughout the Rocky Mountains. By whatever name, it is one of the most tame birds to be found in Grand Teton National Park and in this entire region.

The Gray Jay is the only gray-colored Jay in North America. It is larger and more full bodied than a Robin, gray—of course—with a black or blackish head and a white forehead. The sexes look alike, but youngsters are uniformly sooty, dark above. The Gray Jay will take and eat or cache not only food but also small non-edibles it finds attractive. It greets you at summer cook-outs or in mid-winter when you are out with a sandwich and a thermos. It will fly around your camp or around you on your walk, making short flights from branch to branch to ground to stub to branch. The Gray Jay can shriek like a bird of prey or make a mellow whistle or *cluck* like a Robin. A delightful bird.

Gray Jays nest early in the year, as early as March. Juvenile birds are quite blackish, with a faint white whisker.

LOCAL LOOK-ALIKES The Gray Jay suggests an overgrown Chickadee but is very much larger. In fact, it is almost unmistakable.

© JACKIE GILMORE

CLARK'S NUTCRACKER
Nucifraga columbiana

BEST BET Throughout the whitebark and limber pine forests and around camping areas. A forest and mountainside bird. In winter and spring in settlements, especially Moose, Wilson, and Jackson.

COMMENTS Clark's Nutcracker was called Clark's Crow for a long time, after Captain William Clark who first recorded it not far away in present-day Idaho. Clark's Nutcracker looks something like and in many ways acts like a crow, but it is smaller—perhaps thirteen inches long as opposed to twenty—grayer, and sports distinctive identifying white patches on black wings and tail. It *walks* rather than hops. Its voice is gutteral. In late summer and fall it has been observed above tree line eating the abundant grasshoppers. This bird is sometimes still called Clark's Crow by old-timers in Jackson Hole.

The name Nutcracker comes from the distinctive manner in which this bird chisels pine cones open with its long sharp bill to extract individual pine seeds. The seeds are then rattled and judged as to edibility. Clark's Nutcracker has a throat pouch, an expandible sac, in front of and below its tongue for storing large numbers of seeds—up to 180 whitebark pine seeds. And with all that it can still gather and eat other seeds, call, and do its other important chores. Eventually, these temporarily stored seeds are cached on south facing slopes or on windswept ridges or in places where snow melts early and they can be retrieved and eaten. Since some seeds will inevitably go uneaten, some of them will germinate and grow. Clusters of uniformly aged whitebark and limber pine trees can be detected throughout Grand Teton National Park and in surrounding forests.

LOCAL LOOK-ALIKES Clark's Nutcracker resembles the Gray Jay and the Crow. The Crow has a black body rather than gray, and the Gray Jay lacks the white patches in its gray-black wings and blackish tail.

© THOMAS D. MANGELSEN

BLACK-BILLED MAGPIE
Pica pica

BEST BET Open ranch and grass areas bordered by willows and cottonwoods; sagebrush and foothills. Often seen on roadways after carrion, but just as frequently seen walking in search of insects. Best bet is in open country and along most roads and in towns.

COMMENTS The Black-billed Magpie is a large black and white bird with an exceptionally long, wedge-shaped tail. When seen up close, this foot and a half long bird is iridescent greenish-black, especially on its tail. In flight, white wing patches seem to appear, then disappear. The Black-billed Magpie is a bird species that should not be easily mistaken for any other, with its pattern of black and white, its distinctive, undulating flight, and its silhouette resembling either a prehistoric flying dinosaur or an intercontinental bomber. Moreover, it hops, walks, and struts. Only when perched does it sometimes resemble a Raven or Jay or Clark's Nutcracker, especially if its tail is hidden by shrubbery.

The Black-billed Magpie is a year-long permanent resident of the entire region, except perhaps for isolated mountaintops, which it may not choose to visit.

LOCAL LOOK-ALIKES A second look should make identification of the Black-billed Magpie conclusive.

©JACKIE GILMORE

COMMON RAVEN
Corvus corax

BEST BET At home in this area. In the mountains, in the forests, on the sagebrush steppes, over the lakes, along the rivers, in the towns, and on the ranches. On any day, all year long. If you simply haven't seen one, go to a landfill.

COMMENTS The Common Raven is the ubiquitous big black bird of western North America. Over two feet in length and with a wingspread of four feet or more, it is almost completely ebony. It is not, however, a blackbird; it is in the same scientific family as jays and crows.

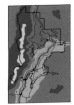

Common Ravens are fun to watch. In the air, they soar or sail, they fly in slow and measured fashion or in rapid flight. They will swoop or coast, they will dive with half-closed wings, they will barrel-roll and spiral. Ravens often ride a gale or a thermal, apparently just in the joy of flight.

Especially in spring and especially in courtship, Ravens will perform spectacular aerobatics, twisting, rolling sideways, chasing each other, turning somersaults, even touching wingtips and feet while one of the pair flies upside down.

The Common Raven walks or hops when on the ground. The walk is measured and stately; the hop is awkward.

The Raven eats almost anything, from carrion to their fresh killed small mammals and birds, to eggs and small vertebrates, to insects, to some vegetation, to garbage. The Common Raven has a loud, hoarse call note, a deep grunt, deep bell-like tones, and various creaks and croaks. There is also a softer kind of self-satisfied *cluck-cluck-cluck.*

LOCAL
LOOK-ALIKES The Common Crow is also all-over black and large—about twenty inches long—but it has a rather squared-off tail. The Common Raven's tail is distinctly wedge-shaped. Crows almost never sail or soar, but must constantly flap their wings. Crows are not common in the Jackson Hole area.

© FRANZ CAMENZIND

MOUNTAIN CHICKADEE
Parus gambeli

BEST BET — Widespread, but especially in the conifers on the mountainsides in summer. In winter and early spring the Mountain Chickadee frequents the valley floor and the towns; check bird feeding stations.

COMMENTS — The Mountain Chickadee is a little bird, sparrow-size or smaller, with a black cap, a gray back, and gray sides. Its black head shows distinctive white eyebrow stripes.

Chickadees are vigorous feeders, bounding from branch to limb to trunk to shrub to branch, searching upright or upside down for insects, or perched to attack an evergreen cone. While not exactly fearless, they don't seem to object to being watched and will call often, revealing their presence. They will call even at fifty degrees below zero in the dead of winter, if it is a sunny day. The song is three clear whistled notes, *fee-bee-bee,* and the note is a husky *cheeks-a-dee-zee-dee.*

About half the chickadees in Grand Teton National Park and its surrounding forests are Mountain Chickadees. The others are Black-capped Chickadees. No fair just alternating your identification . . .

LOCAL LOOK-ALIKES — The Black-capped Chickadee is almost identical in behavior, even in voice, to the Mountain Chickadee, but it has a solid black cap and is rusty on the sides, not gray.

©JEFF FOOTT

A M E R I C A N   D I P P E R   (W A T E R   O U Z E L)
Cinclus mexicanus

BEST BET
Found on all the small, fast creeks in the region during summer. In winter the American Dipper will forage along the Snake and Gros Ventre Rivers. On Cascade Creek near Hidden Falls, on Fish Creek near Wilson.

COMMENTS

The American Dipper is an admirable little bird, a plump package of only eight inches, one of whose chief charms is that it sings all year, even on those blustery mid-winter days when you will not even want to think about the wind-chill factor. The song is cheerful, melodius, trilly, and repetitious, and it carries well over rushing water. The note is a single *zreet.*

The Dipper will be found along the water and, in fact, in it. It plunges into the water and walks on the bottom in search of aquatic insects, invertebrates, and even small fish. On emerging, it often pauses momentarily on a rock and bobs up and down. As it does so, it flashes its white eyelid. Against the dark gray body, this white flash is eaily discernible in field glasses. The Dipper's body is uniformly dark and wren-shaped, and the legs are sturdy. The Dipper reminds one of a short, tailless, colorless Robin determined to go for a swim.

LOCAL
LOOK-ALIKES
Can hardly be mistaken for any other bird in the region, especially if it is seen casually walking into a fast riffle and coming up yards away, bobbing up and down, and bone dry.

© THOMAS D. MANGELSEN

MOUNTAIN BLUEBIRD
Sialia currucoides

BEST BET
Where the sagebrush meets the riverbottoms or the piedmont forests. The National Elk Refuge is always a good Mountain Bluebird haunt. In the Grand Teton National Park areas around the town of Kelly. In the South Park area south of Jackson.

COMMENTS
This beautiful little thrush returns early in spring, sometimes showing up in the southern portion of the Jackson Hole area in February, when there is still a lot of winter to come. Even in a snowstorm, the males (which usually migrate north ahead of the females) are strikingly blue—cerulean or sky-blue all over except for white on the belly. Females are bluish gray above, gray below.

The Mountain Bluebird perches on exposed posts, or on sagebrush, on bitterbrush, in trees—wherever it can get a good view of the various insects that constitute most of its diet. It often hovers close to the ground for the same purpose.

In spring and early summer these welcome migrants and nesters will sing a soft, short warble at and after dawn. The note is a short, soft *chur*. Later in the year, Mountain Bluebirds become almost silent. At that season, they move about in little family groups or more, ranging to the mountain passes in search of insect hatches or of fruits.

LOCAL
LOOK-ALIKES
Although the Mountain Bluebird has a distinctive thrush shape, it should not be easily taken for any of the several other thrushes also found in the Grand Teton National Park region. The thrushes are brownish, or black in the case of the Robins. The Western Bluebird has red on its breast and is rare here.

The male Indigo Bunting has a strong resemblance to the Mountain Bluebird but it has *brown wing bars* and a thick, seed-eating bill; the Indigo Bunting is accidental in this area. The Townsend's Solitaire looks like the female Mountain Bluebird, but it has white sides on its tail, a white eye ring, and buffy wing patches.

©JEFF FOOTT

YELLOW WARBLER
Dendroica petechia

BEST BET Almost everywhere where anything deciduous grows. Riverbottoms and quaking aspen in the forests. In Jackson and Moose and Wilson.

COMMENTS Well named, the Yellow Warbler is essentially all yellow, above as well as below. In common with all warblers, this one is an active little thin-billed tyke, four or five inches long. Since most warblers prefer to live and feed in trees and shrubs, they are generally called "wood warblers," even though they don't warble. Instead, they sing. Exuberantly and well. The Yellow Warbler's song is variable, but it is built around a series of seven insistent, cheerful, sweet notes: a *dee dee dee-ll-dee-ll-dee!*

This is one of the most common birds in the region, in its preferred habitat. It nests close to houses, if it chooses, and all along the rivers and those streams with shrubs or trees on their shores. Close observation reveals that the male Yellow Warbler has reddish streaks on its breast, while the female generally does not show these marks, and that both have yellow even in their tails.

It happens that this high mountain valley has relatively few commonly occuring warblers compared to most regions of the United States. The Jackson Hole-Grand Teton Bird Checklist records only five warblers to be abundant or common. Fortunately, there are a lot of Yellow Warblers to liven things up. They can be heard and seen in the town of Jackson all summer, even on the most frantic of tourist days.

LOCAL LOOK-ALIKES None of the other warblers that occur in the Grand Teton National Park area have yellow tail spots. One exception is the female American Redstart, which shows brown and white along with yellow in wings and tail. The Redstart is uncommon in the area and has not been known to nest. The female Wilson's Warbler does not show yellow tail spots. The American Goldfinch has a black tail and black wings.

©JEFF ROOT

YELLOW-RUMPED WARBLER
Dendroica coronata

BEST BET   A summer resident, a spring and fall migrant. Found nesting mainly in the piedmont and morainal forests and the mountainside forests in the conifers. In migration, Yellow-rumped Warblers will be found all over the valley floor, except in the sagebrush itself.

COMMENTS   You'd never guess how this little five inch wood warbler got its moniker. The rump is bright *yellow* and is pretty visible, even when the bird is perched. The male is blue-gray above and has white on the outer tail feathers, large white wing patches, and black breast marks. Identification of the male Yellow-rump of the west, which was formerly known as Audubon's Warbler, is clinched by his yellow throat. If perchance your bird has a white throat, it is a Myrtle Warbler—and is rare in this region. Kindly notify the nearest friendly local birder. Until the recent revision of the American Ornithological Union that combined these two warblers with yellow behinds into the Yellow-rumped Warbler, birdwatchers were seeing Audubon's Warbler (common here) and, on occasion, Myrtle Warbler (rare here). Many birders still think they are. The females of both these types are brown above and have two wing bars, not patches.

Yellow-rumped Warblers will feed in trees or on the ground, will catch insects in mid-air, and will even eat seeds and fruits when insects get scarce in the fall. They nest in the National Park ecosystem and migrate through in significant numbers, spring and fall. In those migrations the birds seem to be almost everywhere, making their soft call note, a *tsup*. The song is thin, starting with a couple of slow notes followed by a tumble of short notes. This little bird's song is a difficult one; identification by sight is more reliable for most birdwatchers.

LOCAL LOOK-ALIKES   In one sense, all little wood warblers look alike. But no other locally found warbler species has a yellow throat, a yellow rump, and all that white in the wings and tail.

The yellow throat distinguishes the western Yellow-rumped Warbler from the white-throated race, the Myrtle Warbler.

WESTERN TANAGER
Piranga ludoviciana

BEST BET — Open woodlands, usually in the tree canopy. The trails to Phelps and Taggart Lakes in Grand Teton National Park, Moose-Wilson Road, around Slide Lake in the Gros Ventre Mountains, in the piedmont forests where the trees are not in dense stands.

COMMENTS — This six to seven inch bird is the most tropical appearing species to be found in the Rocky Mountain region. The male Western Tanager is yellow with a *red* face and a black back, black wings with yellow wing bars, and a black tail. (In autumn, the red is mostly lost.) The female—which is larger than the male—also has the yellow or white wing bars and is dull greenish above, dull yellowish below. The Tanager bill is short, stout, thick, and somewhat yellowish.

This Tanager nests in this region, but suitable habitat is somewhat scarce and it is always pleasant to come upon this species in summer and fall. Not infrequently in this region, the Western Tanager stages spectacular spring migrations. When this occurs, in May and early June, the birds are just about everywhere where there are trees and shrubs. It is not unusual to see hundreds—even in places such as downtown Jackson—during these migrations.

The Western Tanager has a soft *tu-weep* note, and a song that is Robin-like in quality. The note and a rapid chatter are frequently given, especially in spring and early summer.

LOCAL LOOK-ALIKES — In this region, Scarlet Tanagers make yearly appearances in the spring by ones and twos; but males are all-over scarlet except for black tail and wings. Females are similar to female Western Tanagers but do not have wing bars.

The female Northern (Bullock's) Oriole has white wing bars and a noticeably sharp, pointed bill.

GREEN-TAILED TOWHEE
Pipilo chlorurus

BEST BET In open areas, brushy and rocky hillsides, and throughout the sagebrush flats all the way from the valley floor up almost to the alpine zone. Snow King Mountain, Blacktail Butte, Slide Lake, Taggart Lake trail, and Signal Mountain.

COMMENTS This finch is one of the lesser known bird species in the Jackson Hole environment. Seems a shame, for this is a relatively large (to seven and a quarter inches in length) well-marked songbird (pure white throat with gray breast below and a rufous cap above). Upper parts are a dull olive-green when seen in good sunlight and at close range.

"Close range" meant too close one time for us. A Green-tailed Towhee came out of some roadside lodgepole pine, flying low and directly across the highway and onto the radiator of our car. It is yellow green on the tail and back, and the underwings are quite yellowish as I can now attest. However, this is not my recommendation on how to birdwatch I can assure you, dear reader.

Green-tailed Towhees sing an attractive song, which is given incessantly around the beginning of celestial summer. They sing from the top of a sagebrush or rabbitbrush, the tip of a subalpine fir, or from a rock reposing on an exposed, treeless slope. Their song is a variable melody, beginning with a *whee-churr* followed by high notes, a *burr*, and completed with a weak trill. Their call is a *mew*, their note is a *chink*.

Despite their appearance, song and calls, these Towhees can be easily overlooked. They don't appear to scratch the ground as much as other towhee species do while they search for seeds and insects. I recommend a little scratching and searching on your part for this one. It's worth it.

LOCAL LOOK-ALIKES The Green-tailed Towhee has a superficial resemblance to other ground-hugging birds of the open brushy areas. But no other bird really looks like this robust, common bird of the region.

© ERWIN AND PEGGY BAUER

CHIPPING SPARROW
Spizella passerina

BEST BET
Close to the ground and in open areas. Around Wilson, Moose, and Kelly. In and around the Gros Ventre Campground, and in open tree and shrub-bordered meadows on the road to Two Ocean Lake, both in Grand Teton National Park.

COMMENTS
Far be it for me to question the big time bird field guides, but a Chipping Sparrow has to be the smallest five inch bird around. Everything else the field guides say matches. Summer adults have a bright chestnut-brown cap, a white line over the eye, a dark line through the eye, clear grayish-white underparts, and black bill. A dapper little bird, and one not afraid to approach you closely. Almost friendly. But it certainly doesn't seem to be half the length of a Robin.

The "Chippy's" call is a series of short *chip* notes, all on one pitch and given rapidly. It is so monotonous that at times it can be unnoticed as background noise. Chipping Sparrows sing often in late spring and early summer in the Jackson Hole region, and then usually fall silent. Although a common bird here, and a nesting species, it seems to slip away for the winter, almost unnoticed.

LOCAL LOOK-ALIKES
Some unsensitive persons refer to all small, elusive birds as "little brown birds," lumping some of the most interesting of all birds into one indifferent category. They miss a lot.

The Chipping Sparrow is little and brown all right, but its clear breast and rusty cap underlined first with white, then black, are pretty distinctive. The Brewer's Sparrow is also common in the region, but is a bird of the sagebrush and has no rufous on the head. Instead its crown is finely streaked and is a sandy color.

The Clay-colored Sparrow, rare in Jackson Hole, has been seen in wet, grassy areas. It also lacks the reddish cap and its crown is striped. There is also a brown patch over the ear.

Now then, when it comes to juveniles of these and of similarly-sized species, why you might just want to put your binoculars down and contemplate picking some easier hobby. Young sparrows can be just, ah, small brownish sparrows.

© THOMAS D. MANGELSEN

VESPER SPARROW
Pooecetes gramineus

BEST BET An open country bird. All through the sagebrush and hayfield habitat. The National Elk Refuge is an almost sure bet in spring, summer, and early fall.

COMMENTS The Vesper Sparrow is one of the most common birds of the hayfields, pastures, and sagebrush of Jackson Hole and its surrounding lower foothills. And it is one of the most readily identifiable "little brown birds" because it displays white outer feathers on its dark brown notched tail when it flies up from the ground, where it feeds on seeds and insects. Pretty big for a sparrow, the Vesper Sparrow is about five and a half inches long. It has a white eye ring and, when perched, shows a chestnut-brown shoulder and streaks on the under parts.

The Vesper Sparrow's song is quite lovely, beginning with two clear, long notes followed by two higher ones, and ending in a series of musical trills; it is similar in quality and pattern to the Song Sparrow's song. John Burroughs, a turn-of-the-century naturalist and writer, gave this bird its popular name because he felt it sings more sweetly as evening approaches. It does seem to sing later in the day than do most sparrows, but the song is mellow and clear at dawn and throughout the day. To this writer anyway.

LOCAL LOOK-ALIKES A number of birds that live close to the earth sport white outer tail feathers; there must be some survival mechanism operating thereby. In this region, the Western Meadowlark is found, but it is much larger and stockier. The American Water Pipit *walks*, and bobs its tail, has a very thin bill. The Dark-eyed Junco has white outer tail feathers but is slate-gray in coloration. The Horned Lark has inconspicuous white outer tail feathers, walks rather than hops, and has a black face patch and "horns."

The Lark Sparrow occurs in the region. It is a large, open-country sparrow with a "quail" head pattern, a clear breast with a central spot, and white in the *corners* of the tail. Any Longspur is accidental in the Grand Teton country and an appearance causes a lot of excitement among local birders. If you see one, contact a local and see for yourself.

© THOMAS D. MANGELSEN

WHITE-CROWNED SPARROW
Zonotrichia leucophrys

BEST BET
Along the shores of Jackson and Jenny Lakes, in Colter Bay Campground, in the Gros Ventre Mountains, and wherever there are forest openings with understories of shrubs; frequently in brushy irrigation ditch edges.

COMMENTS
The White-crowned Sparrow is a large sparrow, sprightly and alert in general appearance. This is not the sulking, furtive, and elusive kind of small brownish bird that can frustrate even the experienced birdwatcher. The adult White-crowned Sparrow is streaked prominently with white and black on the top of its head and has brown wings and back, an unstreaked gray breast, and (usually) a pinkish bill. In the immature bird, the crown is striped with beige and dark brown. The song is a wheezy whistle followed by a couple of trills. The call is a *chink*, heard as the birds keep track of each other while foraging on and near the ground.

There are two races of this species in the Rocky Mountains. The adult Mountain White-crown has white eye lines that start from the eye. In the adult Gambel's White-crown, the white eye lines start from the bill. Whether either of these White-crown races dominates in Grand Teton National Park, or if both races even occur here regularly, is not yet known. Birders are encouraged to indicate on their returned checklists which race has been identified, when possible.

LOCAL LOOK-ALIKES
The White-throated Sparrow has a conspicuous white throat, a really black bill, and a yellow spot in front of the eye; White-throats are unusual to rare in the western United States. There are a dozen other Sparrows in the region, none of which should be confused with a well-marked White-crowned Sparrow.

© FRANZ CAMENZIND

DARK-EYED JUNCO
Junco hyemalis

BEST BET The Junco form that occurs in this area seems to prefer grassy openings in stands of conifers and mixed woods. Wander along the Snake River near Moose or Schwabacher's Landing, or take the trails around Two Ocean Lake in Grand Teton National Park; hike through the underbrush along the creeks in Bridger-Teton National Forest. A common nesting species, and in some light winters, the bird might be found at fortunate feeding stations in the settlements.

COMMENTS To the many birdwatchers who keep track of the species they have identified in the field, the recent decision of the American Ornithological Union to lump four species into one—the Dark-eyed Junco—was doubly disappointing. Not only did many of them "lose" three birds, but most truly believed they could separate them by appearance and habitat. Around here, the new designation affected primarily the Oregon or Pink-sided Junco and the occasional Slate-colored and Gray-headed Juncos showing up in migration or in winter. (Most local birders still make separate sub-species identifications.)

Juncos are gray, sparrow-sized and shaped birds with conspicuous white outer tail feathers. The form most common in the Jackson Hole region is black-headed with rusty-pink sides and pinkish bills. The female has a gray head, not black, and a gray hood.

The Junco nests on the ground and, when you saunter nearby, will call nervously in a series of *snit snit* notes. The song is a simple but pleasant trill, varying in pitch and tempo.

LOCAL LOOK-ALIKES The American Ornithological Union's present classification takes some of the sport away. But, the Gray-headed Junco has a light-gray head and sides and a rufous back. Its bill is pale.

The Slate-colored Junco has a gray body, and so is all-over gray, without rufous or brown areas. The White-winged Junco has *two* white wing bars. These two forms are rare in this region.

© THOMAS D. MANGELSEN

WESTERN MEADOWLARK
Sturnella neglecta

BEST BET
In the sageflats or hayfields. Jackson Hole Airport, Antelope Flats, National Elk Refuge, ranches near Moran. Seldom in deep forests.

COMMENTS
This true blackbird is brown and yellow and has white outer tail feathers; what black there is is confined to a broad "V" on the yellow breast. Nevertheless, the Western Meadowlark is one of eight blackbirds normally found in Grand Teton National Park and its surroundings.

The Western Meadowlark is a stocky brownish bird of the open sage and grass. It *walks,* constantly flicking its tail, revealing white outer feathers. In flight, usually low over the ground, rapid beats of short wings alternate with brief sails. The white outer tail feathers are usually conspicuous. The Meadowlark seems to like to sing—and can be heard singing throughout the year—and chooses a conspicuous spot from which to give its variable flute-like version of "Salt Lake City . . . is a very fine city." The bird's call note is a sharp and loud *chuck.*

The Western Meadowlark is Wyoming's official state bird, but it is more commonly found elsewhere in the state where plains and prairies predominate. It does nest in Grand Teton National Park, usually migrating early in the fall, returning again in April.

LOCAL
LOOK-ALIKES
The Eastern Meadowlark is nearly identical, and is best distinguished from the Western Meadowlark by its clear, whistled, much shorter song: "Salt Lake Ci-ty." Other ground birds in the Grand Teton National Park region that show white outer tail feathers—Vesper Sparrow, Dark-eyed Junco, Horned Lark, and Water Pipit—are very much smaller and much less stocky.

YELLOW-HEADED BLACKBIRD
Xanthocephalus xanthocephalus

BEST BET Only where there is water, especially marshes and sloughs. Willow Flats, Christian Pond, Flat Creek at the north end of the town of Jackson, the National Elk Refuge, wet areas in the southern end of Jackson Hole. Many birdwatchers miss seeing this bird but it's here all spring, summer, and fall.

COMMENTS In a flight of mixed blackbirds, these are the big robust ones with the white wing patches. The male Yellow-headed Blackbird is Robin-sized; in spring and summer it has a deep yellow head and breast. The female is smaller and browner, looking almost like a different species, but a dull yellow on the breast and throat can be seen at close range.

If you see one Yellow-headed Blackbird, you will probably see a bunch—one is seldom found all by itself. It is likely, though, that you will hear these birds of the cattails first. The call is harsh and rattling. The song is also harsh and croaking, starting with a couple of notes and ending with a jumble of sounds and squeals. It sounds a lot like a barnyard rooster with a sore throat.

LOCAL LOOK-ALIKES The *white* wing patch—and, in season, the bright yellow marks—distinguish this bird from the other true blackbirds.

ROSY FINCH
Leucosticte arctoa

BEST BET

In summer, Rosy Finches are found in the upper elevations of the region, on the high mountainsides, and in the alpine zone. In winter and spring large flocks of Rosy finches are occasionally found on the valley floor and around feeding stations. Best bet in summer is around the tram station near the top of Rendezvous Mountain in Teton Village. In winter, they are found sporadically in Jackson and South Park.

COMMENTS

There are two local forms of the Rosy Finch which can be found—and readily distinguished—in the greater Teton region. The Gray-crowned Rosy Finch form is a dark brown sparrow-sized bird, with a light gray patch on the back of the head, and a pinkish wash on the rump and wings. Females are duller and often lack the gray patch.

The Black Rosy Finch form is also about six inches in overall length with a black body. The black makes the pinkish wash and gray crown patch more prominent. Voices of both forms are much alike, a short twitter, a high-pitched *zee-o,* and a song which in its chirping closely resembles the House Sparrow (English Sparrow).

Until the 1983 American Ornithological Union Checklist of North American Birds appeared, the two Rosy Finch forms were considered to be separate species. A lot of birdwatchers will continue to do so. The search among the snowfields and talus slopes for the hyper-active finch that walks rather than hops, is a rewarding kind of birdwatching. When found above tree line the bird seems most often to be a Black Rosy Finch form. In spring, what always seems to be mixed flocks of the two former species can often be found. Adoption of the new classification and the lumping of both local forms into Rosy Finch in this book does not imply approval.

LOCAL
LOOK-ALIKES

Obviously the Gray-crowned Rosy Finch looks a lot like the Black Rosy Finch and vice versa, except for the distinction between their black and chestnut-brown bodies.

© THOMAS D. MANGELSEN

CASSIN'S FINCH
Carpodacus cassinii

BEST BET   Stands of pine forests on the mountainsides. Two Ocean Lake, Colter Bay, and Moose in Grand Teton National Park. Throughout the mountains surrounding Jackson Hole, and common in the Mt. Leidy Highlands.

COMMENTS   The Cassin's Finch is one of the most cheerfully alert birds which enliven the sights and sounds of the Grand Teton National Park region. Males are big, brownish, sparrow-like birds, six to six and a half inches long. They have pale reddish breasts, and a squarish red crown patch which ends sharply against the brown nape. The rump is usually a very pale red, and the tail has a distinct fork. The female Cassin's Finch is even more like a big brown sparrow. It has narrowly streaked underparts on a whitish belly, a distinct face pattern, and a robust bill. The two wing bars are indistinct, and the wings reach two-thirds down the tail.

Both sexes of this attractive species sing—a spritely, lively, variable warble. They are silent in winter, which some occasional birds spend on the valley floor around settlements. Their songs are exceedingly welcome when spring finally begins to be suspected after the long winter.

LOCAL LOOK-ALIKES   Partly because it was once called "Cassin's Purple Finch," and partly because the Cassin's strongly resembles the Purple Finch, some confusion occurs every spring when flocks of finches migrate into and through the region. To date, there has not been a confirmed Purple Finch recorded; perhaps a reader of this book will make himself immortal. Purple Finch males are all-over raspberry red, even on the breast and belly. Female Purples have a heavy jaw stripe and a whitish eye stripe. The song is sweeter than that of the Cassin's Finch—and distinctly similar.

The House Finch's song resembles that of the Cassin's Finch too, but is more strident and ends in a harsh *wheer*. It is redder than the Cassin's, especially on the breast and rump. It has a stubbier bill. A few House Finches have been detected in the region. It will reward the birdwatcher, whatever his level of interest, to look carefully at all the "little brown birds" of Jackson Hole.

© THOMAS D. MANGELSEN

RED CROSSBILL
Loxia curvirostra

BEST BET Somewhat unpredictable, but you have to be where there are some conifers. Along the trails through the mountains, along the riverbottoms. Around Moose, around Two Ocean Lake, Colter Bay Nature Trail, and near Lizard Creek Campground.

COMMENTS The Red Crossbill is almost never found far from conifers. Its major food source is conifer seeds, which it pries out of cones with its specialized bill—long and narrow with crossed tips. The adult male is brick-red, brighter on the rump. The female is greenish, with a yellowish rump. This sparrow-sized bird has a big head and a short tail.

Red Crossbills are active, noisy birds, often found in small groups. Their actions are parrot-like: they climb about in the evergreen trees often using both their feet and their bills, often hanging upside down. Their call is a sharp *pip-jip-pip,* repeated two or three times, and a high-pitched trill. Songs are varied but are usually based on a short ascending phrase followed by a trill.

LOCAL LOOK-ALIKES White-winged Crossbill is accidental in the Grand Teton area, according to present records. The male is rosy red, not brick-red, and has conspicuous white wing bars. The female is gray and also has white wing bars.

The crossed mandibles distinguish Crossbills from all other birds in the region.

© ERWIN AND PEGGY BAUER

PINE SISKIN
Carduelis pinus

BEST BET — Seldom far from conifers, except in dandelion season. In spring and early summer, fields of dandelions may harbor flocks of Pine Siskins; look around settlements and ranchlands. In other seasons, your best bet is in the evergreen forests, on Teton and Togwotee Passes, and on most of the trails in Grand Teton National Park. If any Siskins do winter here, they will often be found at bird feeders.

COMMENTS — The Pine Siskin is a five inch, uniformly striped, dark finch with a narrow, pointed bill. The sexes are alike. The birds have really pretty touches of yellow in their wings and at the base of their tail, but these are not always evident, nor always present. The yellow is dandelion-yellow, and when flocks of Pine Siskin rise from a feast of dandelion buds and leaves it's as though some of the petals have taken wing.

Pine Siskins do travel in flocks, not infrequently with other finch species. What are evidently non-breeding birds can be seen in small groups all summer. This is one of the birds more often heard than seen. The song is like that of the American Goldfinch, like a hoarse canary's. The calls are loud; one is a *klee-ip* and the other is a penetrating *zreeee* which rises in pitch. This latter call is unique. When you learn it and then hear it, you can be sure a Pine Siskin made it, even if the songster is somewhere in a dense conifer eighty feet above you.

LOCAL LOOK-ALIKES — Pine Siskins often travel in the company of American Goldfinches, Redpolls, and Red Crossbills.

American Goldfinch in summer are mostly yellow with black or blackish wings. Winter goldfinch are unstreaked. Goldfinch bills are conical, not pointed.

Redpolls do not have yellow in their tails or wings, and are only lightly streaked on their breasts.

Young Red Crossbills are striped all over, but have distinctive crossed mandibles.

© THOMAS D. MANGELSEN

AMERICAN GOLDFINCH
Carduelis tristis

BEST BET In open country where weedy undergrowth occurs. Not in the sagebrush steppe but along the roads and irrigation ditches in the southern end of the valley. The Fall Creek Road from south Wilson has many thistles along its edges, a weed favored by the American Goldfinch.

COMMENTS The "wild canary" with the typical finch shape and an exaggerated finch-like undulatory flight pattern. The American Goldfinch calls often in flight, celebrating each dip with a *pee-dee-o-ree* call. The song is canary-like, a prolonged series of twitters and trills, punctuated with relatively harsh *szee* notes.

The male American Goldfinch is a small (four and a half inch to five and a half inch) yellow bird with black wings, tail and forehead. The female is a dull yellow, darker above, with blackish wings and two wing bars. The bills of both sexes are conical, yellowish or light-colored, and short and small for a finch.

Canada, bull, and bristle thistles have become commonplace exotic plants in the Jackson Hole region since the mid-1970's. In the southern end of the valley, these thistles now thrive and, in response to this food source, the goldfinch is commonly found in that portion of the region. The bird now regularly winters in the valley in small numbers relying on bird feeders during the harshest winter weeks. Winter goldfinch plumages are drab and variable; the dark wings with distinct wing bars and the pale short bills may be the only clues to identification.

LOCAL LOOK-ALIKES The Yellow Warbler is yellowish all over, and does not have black anywhere. The warbler's bill is sharp and slender, not conical.

© THOMAS D. MANGELSEN

EVENING GROSBEAK
Coccothraustes vespertinus

BEST BET — This bird is a vertical migrant. In summer months, go to the higher mountainside conifer forests, Two Ocean Lake, Colter Bay in Grand Teton National Park. In winter, go to the settlements—Jackson, Moose, Wilson, Teton Village.

COMMENTS — The Evening Grosbeak is a big finch (eight inches in length) with a very big, conical, pale bill and a short tail. As a result, it looks chunky or stocky. In flight, the wings look prominently black and white. The male is dull yellow, with a dark head and yellow eye stripe. The female is grayish with traces of yellow, black, and white.

The Evening Grosbeak flies in a characteristically finch-like undulating pattern and almost always in groups. This is a highly gregarious bird, even when nesting. It communicates with single or double loud ringing whistles, a *klee-up-klee-up*. Its song is a short warble, usually ending in a whistle.

This attractively marked, cheerful finch is always a pleasure to come upon. It brightens up the dark green forest trail in summer and it livens up a bleak winter day. People who feed birds always welcome them, even when they empty sunflower trays a half dozen times a day.

LOCAL LOOK-ALIKES — A brightly marked male Evening Grosbeak looks a little like "an overgrown American Goldfinch" (Roger Tory Peterson). The male Pine Grosbeak is longer, has a short *black* bill and less white in the wing. The Snow Bunting has large white wing patches but is shorter by a couple of inches. In the Grand Teton area Snow Buntings are occasional in winter and spring. Buntings seldom come to feeders.

FREE ADVICE

For Whatever That's Worth

ABOUT THE CLIMATE

This high mountain valley and its much higher surroundings doesn't always look as it does in the publicity snapshots. For a few weeks during the year, about the only trouble anyone can get into is getting soaked in a rainstorm or temporarily lost. And there are the mosquitoes. Even on the nicest day in mid-summer, some caution should be exercised. It can get below freezing on any calendar day. It can snow on almost any day; the average growing (frost-free) season on the valley floor is only eighty-plus days. One year it was four days.

The weather during the rest of the year should be considered even more seriously. Those mountainsides covered with snow are pleasant to ski on during the sunny days pictured in calendar art; but that *is* snow. On those days when the snow is falling, one can get lost. And cold—hypothermia is a constant possibility one should never ignore. First snow is usually in September. Winters are long and harsh.

Not to worry too much: we haven't lost *nearly* as many birders as we have mountain climbers, hunters, fishermen, or skiers. Birdwatchers can't be smarter, can they? It must be pure luck, but a little thought before venturing off on a windy, raw day or before sauntering into the hind end of a moose can't hurt.

ABOUT THE WATER

Hate to say it, but it's not worth the risk of giardia to drink out of any lake, river, or creek. Don't do it.

ABOUT ACCOMMODATIONS

There are many dude ranches, hotels, motels, and campgrounds all about. Reservations during peak season—June through August, and around Christmas—are advised. There are campgrounds in Grand Teton National Park and in Bridger-Teton National Forest, and commercial ones in and near Moran, Kelly, and Jackson.

ABOUT ROAD ACCESS

The paved highways shown on area maps are open in late spring, all summer, and fall. Some are not plowed in winter, and some of *those* may be traveled then on skis, snowshoes, or snow machines. When dry, unpaved roads can be traveled, many miles by automobile and other stretches by truck or four-wheel drive vehicles. When wet, it is simply prudent not to go by motor vehicle. When wet, it may not be prudent even to walk across country . . . talk about slippery . . .

ABOUT TRAIL ACCESS

To avoid mud it is best not to follow the snowline in spring too closely, whether on foot, on a horse, or in a vehicle. By July 4, all trails in the area are usually snow free. In the alpine zone, of course, snowfields will be found all year. There are even small glaciers in the Teton Range.

ABOUT WATER ACCESS

The Snake River is navigable and has rafts on it for sightseeing, fishing, and pure recreation. When care is exercised, rafting is quite safe. Tours are available. Some people use dories—pretty safe. Some use canoes—requiring exceptional care; many canoes get wrapped around tree trunks and river rocks. The Snake is a big, fast, cold river. Be cautious; the bottom can be slippery and the current is always strong, even after spring run-off is over and in winter. All the waters in the region are cold and usually fast.

ABOUT THE WEATHER—AGAIN?

Storms can come up rapidly. If you are out on any craft on Jackson, Jenny, or Lower Slide Lakes, keep a weather eye out. If in doubt, get to shore.

ABOUT HUNTING

Hunting is a big deal in Wyoming. Seasons vary, but generally elk, deer, and waterfowl go from September through December. There is a special elk hunt even in portions of Grand Teton National Park. Bear, coyote, mountain lion, rabbit, mountain sheep: hunting is a big deal in Wyoming. If you are out in the forests in the fall, try not to look like a game animal. Something hunter-orange on your head or torso is a good idea. Don't startle a hunter.

Don't startle any other big wild animal either. You may get accidently trampled. Don't get between a mother moose, bear, elk, or cow and its baby. You may then get deliberately trampled.

ABOUT THE ALTITUDE

This is high altitude country. The valley floor is 6,000 feet above sea level at its lowest point. Jackson Lake is at about 6,800 feet. Tree line is around 10,500 feet. The Grand Teton is 13,770 feet. If you are not accustomed to higher elevations, take some time to get acclimatized or, at least, pace yourself. The hospital emergency room is not recommended as a prime birding spot.

ABOUT THE BIRDS

This book discusses only about a sixth of the birds reported to occur in Jackson Hole. A 1984 checklist appears in the book; one is also available at Grand Teton National Park Headquarters and at the Wyoming Game and Fish Department District Office, Bridger-Teton National Forest Headquarters, and the National Elk Refuge Headquarters, all in Jackson. The reports of bird observations, exotics and especially commonly occuring species, made by visitors to Jackson Hole have been of special help in making the bird checklist increasingly accurate. Your cooperation will be welcomed and appreciated. Just fill it out and drop it in the mailbox; no postage is required. Appreciate it.

FINALLY!

If you are a beginning birdwatcher, you should know that birds will avoid noise and commotion. You will see a lot more birds if you and your companions walk quietly and speak softly. So will other observers; respect their stalk of a bird, and they will probably help you in identification.

MORE INFORMATION

Detailed maps of Jackson Hole, Grand Teton National Park, and northwestern Wyoming are available, showing watercourses, paved and unpaved roads, foot and horse trails, and climbing routes. Grand Teton National Park Headquarters in Moose has perhaps the best selection from which to choose, including specialized maps and topographical maps prepared by the U.S. Geological Survey made available through Grand Teton Natural History Association. Maps of Bridger-Teton National Forest can be obtained at Forest headquarters in Jackson. Information concerning the National Elk Refuge can be had at its headquarters, also located in Jackson.

Personnel at these federal agencies are familiar with current road and trail conditions and any restrictions upon ingress. They, and staff at the Wyoming Game and Fish Department district office in Jackson, may have immediate information on particular bird species. Such helpful information is made available when birdwatchers share their interesting sightings both by telling these agencies directly and by filling in and returning (free) copies of the Jackson Hole Bird Checklist. Your cooperation in this latter regard will be appreciated and your data, be assured, will be used in the future.

The Jackson Hole Bird Club, a modest group of amateur and some professional nature students, meets on the second Sunday of each month. Meeting details are announced in advance in the local newspapers and are usually held in Jackson. Visitors are always welcome to attend its meetings and share observations.

CHECKLIST

Jackson Hole is defined, for the purposes of this checklist, as including the western slope of the Gros Ventre Range, the Teton Range and the valley area south of Yellowstone National Park extending to the confluence of the Snake and Hoback Rivers. The area covered includes all of Grand Teton National Park, the National Elk Refuge, the corridor between Yellowstone and Teton Parks and a large portion of the Bridger-Teton National Forest.

Seven primary habitat zones are present in this area: Riverbottoms, Lakes and Ponds, Sageflats, Ranches and Hayfields, Morainal and Piedmont Forests, Mountainsides, Alpine, and Settlements. Elevation varies from approximately 6,000 feet to over 13,000 feet.

As the list indicates, 293 species of birds have been recorded. Surely, more have been and will be observed.

RELATIVE FREQUENCY OF OCCURRENCE

a   ABUNDANT - likely to be seen in large numbers in appropriate habitat and season.

c   COMMON - may be observed most of the time and in good numbers in appropriate habitat and season.

o   OCCASIONAL - occurs irregularly or in small numbers, but in appropriate habitat and season.

r   RARE - unexpected as to season or range.

x   ACCIDENTAL or SURPRISING - out of its range; or recorded only once or twice.

?   VERIFICATION UNAVAILABLE - additional information especially welcome!

SEASONS	BREEDING STATUS
SP March-May	* following species' name indicates nest or dependent young have been observed.
SU June-August	
F September-November	• following species' name indicates only circumstantial evidence of breeding.
W December-February	

NO. SPECIES	SP	SU	F	W
LOONS				
[ ] Arctic Loon			x	
[ ] Common Loon*, p.20	o	o	o	x
GREBES				
[ ] Pied-billed Grebe*	o	o	o	?
[ ] Horned Grebe	r	r	o	
[ ] Red-necked Grebe	x		x	
[ ] Eared Grebe •	c	o	o	
[ ] Western Grebe*, p.21	o	o	o	
PELICANS				
[ ] American White Pelican, p.22	o	o	o	
CORMORANTS				
[ ] Double-crested Cormorant •	o	o	o	
BITTERNS AND HERONS				
[ ] American Bittern*	o	o	o	
[ ] Great Blue Heron*, p.23	c	c	c	o
[ ] Great Egret (Common or American Egret)	x			
[ ] Snowy Egret	o	o	o	
[ ] Little Blue Heron	?			
[ ] Cattle Egret	r			
[ ] Green-backed Heron (Green Heron)	x			
[ ] Black-crowned Night-Heron	x		x	
IBISES				
[ ] White-faced Ibis	o			
WATERFOWL				
[ ] Tundra Swan (Whistling Swan)	x		o	o
[ ] Trumpeter Swan*, p.24	c	c	c	c
[ ] Greater White-fronted Goose			x	
[ ] Snow Goose	o		o	r
[ ] Brant			x	
[ ] Canada Goose*, p.25	c	c	c	c
[ ] Wood Duck	r	r	r	r
[ ] Green-winged Teal*	c	o	c	o
[ ] Mallard*, p.26	a	c	a	c
[ ] Northern Pintail*	o	o	c	c
[ ] Blue-winged Teal	c	o	c	r
[ ] Cinnamon Teal*, p.27	o	o	r	x
[ ] Northern Shoveler*	o	r	o	o
[ ] Gadwall*	c	o	c	o
[ ] Eurasian Wigeon (European Wigeon)	x	x		
[ ] American Wigeon*	c	o	c	r
[ ] Canvasback*	o	r	o	
[ ] Redhead •	o	o	c	

— 83 —

NO. SPECIES	SP	SU	F	W
WATERFOWL *(continued)*				
[ ] Ring-necked Duck*	o	c	c	r
[ ] Greater Scaup		x		
[ ] Lesser Scaup*	o	o	o	
[ ] Harlequin Duck*	o	o	o	
[ ] Surf Scoter		x		
[ ] White-winged Scoter		x		
[ ] Common Goldeneye*	o	o	o	o
[ ] Barrow's Goldeneye*, p.28	c	c	c	o
[ ] Bufflehead*	c	o	c	o
[ ] Hooded Merganser	r		r	o
[ ] Common Merganser*, p.29	c	c	c	c
[ ] Red-breasted Merganser	o		o	?
[ ] Ruddy Duck*	o	o	o	x
VULTURES, HAWKS AND FALCONS				
[ ] Turkey Vulture	r	r	r	
[ ] Osprey*, p.30	c	c	c	
[ ] Black-shouldered Kite *(White-tailed Kite)*			x	
[ ] Bald Eagle*, p.31	c	c	c	c
[ ] Northern Harrier* *(Marsh Hawk)*	o	o	o	r
[ ] Sharp-shinned Hawk*	o	o	o	x
[ ] Cooper's Hawk*	o	o	o	
[ ] Goshawk*	c	c	c	o
[ ] Broad-winged Hawk	x		?	
[ ] Swainson's Hawk*, p.32	c	c	c	
[ ] Red-tailed Hawk*, p.33	c	c	c	r
[ ] Ferruginous Hawk*	r	r	r	
[ ] Rough-legged Hawk	o		c	o
[ ] Golden Eagle*	o	o	o	o
[ ] American Kestrel*, p.34	c	c	c	r
[ ] Merlin •	o	r	o	x
[ ] Peregrine Falcon*, p.35	r	r	r	r
[ ] Gyrfalcon	x		x	x
[ ] Prairie Falcon*, p.36	o	o	o	x
GALLINACEOUS BIRDS				
[ ] Gray Partridge*	r	o	o	o
[ ] Chukar •	r	r	r	r
[ ] Blue Grouse*, p.37	c	c	c	c
[ ] Ruffed Grouse*	c	c	c	c
[ ] Sage Grouse*, p.38	c	c	c	c
[ ] Sharp-tailed Grouse		x	x	x
RAILS AND COOTS				
[ ] Virginia Rail		?	x	
[ ] Sora •	o	o	o	
[ ] American Coot*, p.39	o	o	c	r

NO. SPECIES	SP	SU	F	W

CRANES

	SP	SU	F	W
[　] Sandhill Crane*, p.40	c	o	c	
[　] Whooping Crane, p.19 and p.40	r	r	r	

PLOVERS

	SP	SU	F	W
[　] Black-bellied Plover	r		r	
[　] Lesser Golden-Plover	x			
(American Golden Plover)				
[　] Semipalmated Plover	r		r	
[　] Killdeer*, p.41	o	c	c	o
[　] Mountain Plover		x		
[　] Black-necked Stilt		x	x	
[　] American Avocet	o	o	o	
[　] Greater Yellowlegs	o	o	o	
[　] Lesser Yellowlegs	o	o	o	
[　] Solitary Sandpiper	o	r	o	
[　] Willet	o	r	o	
[　] Spotted Sandpiper*, p.42	c	c	c	
[　] Upland Sandpiper		x		
[　] Long-billed Curlew*	o	o	o	
[　] Marbled Godwit	o	r	r	
[　] Red Knot	x		x	
[　] Sanderling	x	r	x	
[　] Semipalmated Sandpiper		r	o	
[　] Western Sandpiper	x	r	o	
[　] Least Sandpiper	o	r	o	
[　] Baird's Sandpiper	r	o	o	
[　] Pectoral Sandpiper			r	
[　] Dunlin	?	x		
[　] Stilt Sandpiper	r			
[　] Long-billed Dowitcher	o	o	o	
[　] Common Snipe*, p.43	c	c	c	
[　] American Woodcock	x	x		

PHALAROPES

	SP	SU	F	W
[　] Wilson's Phalarope*, p.44	c	o	r	
[　] Red-necked Phalarope	o		r	
(Northern Phalarope)				

JAEGERS

	SP	SU	F	W
[　] Parasitic Jaeger		x		

GULLS AND TERNS

	SP	SU	F	W
[　] Franklin's Gull	o	o	o	
[　] Bonaparte's Gull	o		r	
[　] Ring-billed Gull	r	o	r	
[　] California Gull, p.45	c	c	c	
[　] Western Gull			x	

GULLS AND TERNS *(continued)*

Species	SP	SU	F	W
[ ] Sabine's Gull			x	
[ ] Caspian Tern	r	o	o	
[ ] Common Tern			r	r
[ ] Forster's Tern	x	r	r	
[ ] Black Tern	o	o	o	
[ ] Ancient Murrelet			x	

DOVES AND CUCKOOS

Species	SP	SU	F	W
[ ] Rock Dove •	o	o	o	o
[ ] Band-tailed Pigeon	x	x	?	?
[ ] Mourning Dove*	o	o	o	x
[ ] Black-billed Cuckoo	o	o	o	x
[ ] Yellow-billed Cuckoo		x	x	

OWLS

Species	SP	SU	F	W
[ ] Common Barn Owl			x	
[ ] Flammulated Owl			x	
[ ] Western Screech-Owl •	r	r	r	r
[ ] Great Horned Owl*, p.46	o	o	o	o
[ ] Snowy Owl			x	x
[ ] Northern Hawk Owl		?		
[ ] Northern Pigmy Owl •	r	r	r	r
[ ] Burrowing Owl	r	r	r	
[ ] Barred Owl			x	
[ ] Great Gray Owl*, p.47	o	o	o	o
[ ] Long-eared Owl*		o	o	x
[ ] Short-eared Owl*	r	o	o	r
[ ] Boreal Owl	r	r	r	r
[ ] Northern Saw-whet Owl •	r	r	r	r

NIGHTHAWKS

Species	SP	SU	F	W
[ ] Common Nighthawk*, p.48	c	c	c	
[ ] Common Poorwill	x			

SWIFTS AND HUMMINGBIRDS

Species	SP	SU	F	W
[ ] Black Swift		?		
[ ] White-throated Swift		x		
[ ] Magnificent Hummingbird		x		
(Rivoli's Hummingbird)				
[ ] Black-chinned Hummingbird			o	r
[ ] Calliope Hummingbird*, p.49	c	c	c	
[ ] Broad-tailed Hummingbird*	o	o	o	
[ ] Rufous Hummingbird*	o	o	o	

KINGFISHERS

Species	SP	SU	F	W
[ ] Belted Kingfisher*, p.50	c	c	c	o

NO. SPECIES	SP	SU	F	W
WOODPECKERS				
[ ] Lewis' Woodpecker*	o	o	r	
[ ] Red-headed Woodpecker	x	x		
[ ] Acorn Woodpecker		x		
[ ] Yellow-bellied Sapsucker*	c	c	c	x
[ ] Williamson's Sapsucker*	o	o	r	
[ ] Downy Woodpecker*	c	c	c	c
[ ] Hairy Woodpecker*, p.51	c	c	c	c
[ ] White-headed Woodpecker	x	x		
[ ] Three-toed Woodpecker	o	o	r	?
(Northern Three-toed Woodpecker)*, p.52				
[ ] Black-backed Woodpecker	o	o	o	r
(Black-backed Three-toed Woodpecker)*				
[ ] Northern Flicker *(Common,*	c	c	c	o
Red-shafted and Yellow-shafted Flicker)*, p.53				
[ ] Pileated Woodpecker		x		
FLYCATCHERS				
[ ] Olive-sided Flycatcher*	c	c	c	
[ ] Western Wood-Pewee*, p.54	c	c	c	
[ ] Willow Flycatcher*	o	o	o	
[ ] Least Flycatcher		x		
[ ] Hammond's Flycatcher	o	o	o	
[ ] Dusky Flycatcher*	c	c	c	
[ ] Western Flycatcher •	o	o	o	
[ ] Say's Phoebe	r	r	r	
[ ] Great Crested Flycatcher			x	
[ ] Western Kingbird	r	r	r	
[ ] Eastern Kingbird	o	o	o	
LARKS				
[ ] Horned Lark •	o	o	o	
SWALLOWS				
[ ] Tree Swallow*	a	a	a	
[ ] Violet-green Swallow*	c	c	c	
[ ] Northern Rough-winged Swallow*	o	o	o	
[ ] Bank Swallow*	c	c	c	
[ ] Cliff Swallow*, p.55	a	a	c	
[ ] Barn Swallow*	c	c	c	
JAYS, MAGPIES AND CROWS				
[ ] Gray Jay •, p.56	c	c	c	c
[ ] Steller's Jay*	c	c	c	c
[ ] Pinyon Jay		x	x	
[ ] Clark's Nutcracker*, p.57	c	c	c	c
[ ] Black-billed Magpie*, p.58	c	c	c	c
[ ] American Crow*	o	o	o	o
[ ] Common Raven*, p.59	c	c	c	c

NO. SPECIES	SP	SU	F	W
CHICKADEES				
[ ] Black-capped Chickadee*	c	c	c	c
[ ] Mountain Chickadee*, **p.60**	c	c	c	c
[ ] Plain Titmouse		?		
NUTHATCHES				
[ ] Red-breasted Nuthatch*	c	c	c	c
[ ] White-breasted Nuthatch*	c	c	c	c
[ ] Pygmy Nuthatch			x	
CREEPERS				
[ ] Brown Creeper*	o	o	o	o
WRENS				
[ ] Rock Wren*	o	o	o	o
[ ] House Wren*	c	c	c	
[ ] Winter Wren •	x	r	?	
[ ] Marsh Wren*	c	c	c	
DIPPERS				
[ ] American Dipper, **p.61**	c	c	c	c
KINGLETS AND GNATCATCHERS				
[ ] Golden-crowned Kinglet •	o	o	o	r
[ ] Ruby-crowned Kinglet*	c	c	o	r
[ ] Blue-gray Gnatcatcher	x		x	
THRUSHES				
[ ] Western Bluebird	o		o	
[ ] Mountain Bluebird*, **p.62**	c	c	c	
[ ] Townsend's Solitaire*	c	c	o	o
[ ] Veery •	o	o	o	
[ ] Swainson's Thrush*	c	c	o	
[ ] Hermit Thrush*	c	c	o	
[ ] American Robin*	a	a	a	r
[ ] Varied Thrush			r	x
MOCKINGBIRDS AND THRASHERS				
[ ] Gray Catbird •	o	o	r	
[ ] Northern Mockingbird		x	x	
[ ] Sage Thrasher*	o	o	o	
PIPITS				
[ ] Water Pipit •	c	c	c	r
[ ] Sprague's Pipit	x		x	
WAXWINGS				
[ ] Bohemian Waxwing	o		r	o
[ ] Cedar Waxwing	o	o	o	o

NO.	SPECIES	SP	SU	F	W
	SHRIKES				
[ ]	Northern Shrike	o		o	o
[ ]	Loggerhead Shrike •	o	r		o
	STARLINGS				
[ ]	European Starling*	c	c	c	o
	VIREOS				
[ ]	Solitary Vireo		r	r	
[ ]	Warbling Vireo*	a	a	o	
[ ]	Red-eyed Vireo		o	o	
	WARBLERS				
[ ]	Tennessee Warbler			r	x
[ ]	Orange-crowned Warbler •	o	o	o	
[ ]	Nashville Warbler	x		x	
[ ]	Yellow Warbler*, p.63	a	a	c	
[ ]	Chestnut-sided Warbler			x	
[ ]	Black-throated Blue Warbler				x
[ ]	Yellow-rumped Warbler*, p.64	a	a	c	
[ ]	Townsend's Warbler			r	r
[ ]	Blackburnian Warbler			x	
[ ]	Palm Warbler			x	
[ ]	Bay-breasted Warbler			x	
[ ]	American Redstart	o	o		
[ ]	Prothonotary Warbler			x	
[ ]	Northern Waterthrush	r		r	x
[ ]	MacGillivray's Warbler*	c	c	o	
[ ]	Common Yellowthroat •	c	c	c	
[ ]	Wilson's Warbler •	c	c	c	
[ ]	Yellow-breasted Chat	x	x		
	TANAGERS				
[ ]	Western Tanager*, p.65	c	c	o	
	GROSBEAKS, BUNTINGS, SPARROWS, BLACKBIRDS, ORIOLES AND FINCHES				
[ ]	Rose-breasted Grosbeak	o	x		
[ ]	Black-headed Grosbeak*	o	c	o	
[ ]	Lazuli Bunting*	o	o	r	
[ ]	Indigo Bunting	x	x		
[ ]	Green-tailed Towhee*, p.66	o	c	c	
[ ]	Rufous-sided Towhee	r	r	r	
[ ]	Brown Towhee		x		?
[ ]	American Tree Sparrow	o		o	o
[ ]	Chipping Sparrow*, p.67	c	c	c	?
[ ]	Clay-colored Sparrow*			r	
[ ]	Brewer's Sparrow*	c	c	c	
[ ]	Vesper Sparrow*, p.68	c	c	c	
[ ]	Lark Sparrow			o	o

GROSBEAKS, BUNTINGS, SPARROWS, BLACKBIRDS,
ORIOLES AND FINCHES *(continued)*

		SP	SU	F	W
[ ]	Black-throated Sparrow	x			
[ ]	Sage Sparrow	x	x		
[ ]	Lark Bunting	r	r		
[ ]	Savannah Sparrow •	c	c	c	
[ ]	Grasshopper Sparrow		x		
[ ]	Fox Sparrow*	o	o		
[ ]	Song Sparrow*	c	c	c	o
[ ]	Lincoln's Sparrow*	o	c	c	
[ ]	Swamp Sparrow		x	x	
[ ]	White-throated Sparrow	r		r	
[ ]	Golden-crowned Sparrow	?			
[ ]	White-crowned Sparrow*, p.69	a	a	a	r
[ ]	Harris' Sparrow	r		r	r
[ ]	Dark-eyed Junco *(White-winged,*	a	a	c	o
	Slate-colored, Oregon and				
	Gray-headed Junco), p.70				
[ ]	McCown's Longspur		x		
[ ]	Lapland Longspur	x			x
[ ]	Snow Bunting	x		r	o
[ ]	Bobolink •	o	o		
[ ]	Red-winged Blackbird*	c	c	c	o
[ ]	Western Meadowlark •, p.71	o	o	o	x
[ ]	Yellow-headed Blackbird*, p.72	c	c	c	x
[ ]	Rusty Blackbird			x	
[ ]	Brewer's Blackbird*	c	c	a	o
[ ]	Common Grackle	o	o	o	
[ ]	Brown-headed Cowbird*	c	c	c	
[ ]	Orchard Oriole*	x			
[ ]	Northern Oriole *(Bullock's Oriole)**	o	o	o	
[ ]	Rosy Finch	c	c	o	o
	(Gray-crowned, Black Rosy Finch), p.73				
[ ]	Pine Grosbeak •	o	o	o	o
[ ]	Cassin's Finch*, p.74	c	c	c	o
[ ]	House Finch	x	x	x	x
[ ]	Red Crossbill •, p.75	o	o	o	o
[ ]	White-winged Crossbill	x	x		x
[ ]	Common Redpoll	c		o	o
[ ]	Hoary Redpoll	x			x
[ ]	Pine Siskin*, p.76	c	c	c	o
[ ]	American Goldfinch*, p.77	o	o	o	x
[ ]	Evening Grosbeak*, p.78	c	o	c	c
[ ]	House Sparrow*	c	c	c	c

Checklist compiled by Bert and Meg Raynes, Jackson Hole, Wyoming

NOTES